PRAISE FOR
LETTERS FROM BACKSTAGE

"Not only is *Letters from Backstage* an insider's view of the wacky world of professional theatre that most people never get to see, but it is also an entertaining guide to each of the cities that Michael visits on tour. Interesting places to see, fabulous places to eat, ghost stories, folklore, the quirks of each town, and a vivid picture of the people and diverse culture in the various regions of our country. It can't miss!"—*Lisa Ann Richard, Actress*, Mamma Mia!

"All too often actors take for granted their journey through this elusive and inexplicable business of show. On that rare occasion, one of us (them) gains a perspective on it that is enlightening, introspective, entertaining and filled with humor . . . demystifying and humanizing the experience of what a true professional theatre actor encounters on his particular and personal path. In this time of great concern and debate over what it means to be an American, Michael Kostroff has masterfully chronicled not only life on the road with hit theatrical shows, but life on the road in America, as a proud American actor, speaking frankly, lovingly, and honestly . . . embracing its flaws and lauding its beauty with equal and impassioned reverence. The picture he so cunningly paints of our country and its cast of characters should be seen and heard in every town from Anchorage to Key West, from San Diego to Bangor and everywhere in between."—*Paul Leighton Nygro, Actor*, Reefer Madness

"Michael's tales from the road have become a family tradition in our house. Much like the arrival of the Tooth Fairy, we eagerly await his next exquisite 'touring-actor' adventure. Unfailingly, each episode is enlightening, honest, informative, beautifully written, and most importantly, damn hilarious! Kostroff is a brilliant actor and writer. I think I hate him."—*Billie Shepard, Acting Instructor*, San Francisco

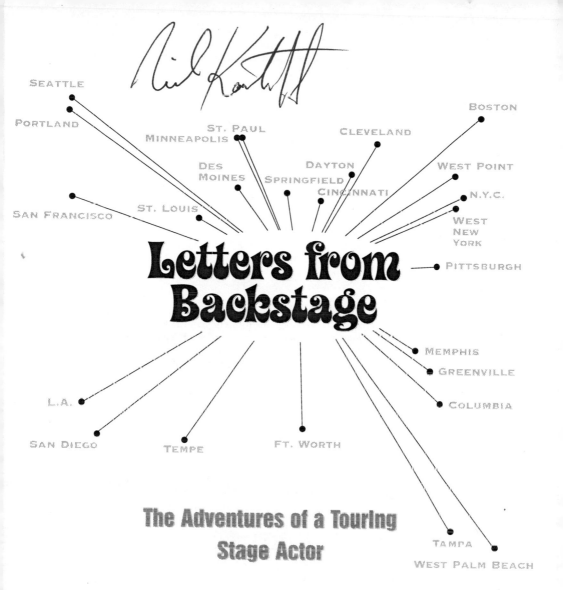

SEATTLE

PORTLAND

ST. PAUL
MINNEAPOLIS

CLEVELAND

BOSTON

DES
MOINES   DAYTON
SPRINGFIELD
CINCINNATI

WEST POINT

N.Y.C.

SAN FRANCISCO   ST. LOUIS

WEST
NEW
YORK

Letters from Backstage

PITTSBURGH

MEMPHIS

GREENVILLE

L.A.

COLUMBIA

SAN DIEGO   TEMPE   FT. WORTH

The Adventures of a Touring Stage Actor

TAMPA

WEST PALM BEACH

MICHAEL KOSTROFF

ALLWORTH PRESS
NEW YORK

09 08 07 06 05   5 4 3 2 1

Published by Allworth Press
An imprint of Allworth Communications, Inc.
10 East 23rd Street, New York, NY 10010

Cover design by Derek Bacchus

Interior design by Mary Belibasakis

Page composition/typography by Integra Software Services, Pvt. Ltd., Pondicherry, India

ISBN-13: 978-1-58115-441-2

Library of Congress Cataloging-in-Publication Data:

Kostroff, Michael.
    Letters from backstage: the adventures of a touring stage actor / Michael Kostroff.
        p. cm.
    Includes index.
    ISBN 1-58115-441-0 (pbk.)
    1. Kostroff, Michael. 2. Actors–United States–Biography. 3. Schönberg, Claude-Michel. Misérables. 4. Brooks, Mel, 1926- Producers. I. Title.

PN2287.K69A3 2005
792.02'8'092—dc22
                                                                        2005019811

DEDICATION

THROUGHOUT MY LIFE, in the best of times and in the worst of times, when I was weird and crazy and when I was wise and strong, when I was broke and when I was rolling in dough, the people who have been with me consistently have always been theatre people. They've been my friends, lovers, teachers, counselors, confidants, sisters and brothers, mothers and fathers, and lots of crazy cousins—in all ways, my true family. It was theatre people who valued me, encouraged me, told me when my work needed work, straightened me out when I was being an ass, ribbed me when I got too serious, and always did so with tolerance and support. Always with my best interests at heart. And often, they seemed to feel I was perfectly great just the way I was. Imagine that.

Theatre people are, as a rule, crazy. Of course we are. The world needs crazy people to make the art. I've come to love and embrace my adopted family for that very quality. God bless us; we're all bananas.

And so this book is dedicated to theatre people everywhere—the folks who put it on and the folks who come to watch it. I thank God we found each other. To have lived and worked among you has been exactly what I wanted from my life.

TABLE OF CONTENTS

FOREWORD

ONE OF THE GREATEST stage comedies I have ever seen is a piece by Michael Frayn entitled, *Noises Off*. It endeavors to depict the onstage shenanigans of a frenzied troupe of performers in an underwhelming provincial comedy/thriller. The mediocre writing and staging of the "onstage" show is funny enough, but the bit of sheer brilliance is the playwright's attempt to show the comedy of errors and tempers and ego that occur backstage, behind the scenes. Mr. Frayn understood to great delight that the show behind the show can often be the most delicious of all.

"Backstage" is the intersection of two completely different worlds: Within the proscenium, flooded with light, is one of the greatest illusions ever devised. A whole world and its inhabitants are alive and vital in an audience's head; none of it real but all of it seen and heard and felt. Yet in the wings, just a few feet away, is another world that the audience is completely unaware of. It is where the real world actually lives—unseen, unheard, and hopefully entirely unthought of. Polar opposites, reversed reality, separated by light and a few pieces of muslin scenery.

For as long as I can remember, I have lived at the edge of these two universes we call "backstage." And before I lived there, I dreamed of it. Because to take residence there is to breathe a most rarified air. It is where every performer endeavors to live. Once there, you stand on the precipice of magic and heightened reality.

There is a great life backstage, filled with excitement and ecstasy; teeming with laughter and sensuality. And yet it has drama and despair in equal abundance. Entire lives can be lived backstage. Or, just the highlights of a lifetime.

The world of "backstage" is not limited to the wings of a single theater. It extends into every theater a performer plays. It even goes beyond those borders. When a performer is traveling on the road, away from the familiar routines of daily life, the entire journey becomes "backstage." Living out of suitcases in temporary lodgings, separated from friends and family, real life seems even further away than the distance traveled. It is a fantasy world, and a magical one at that.

Very few people take the time to appreciate that journey until it is behind them. They miss the history and beauty of the towns they visit. They lose sight of the daily comedies and tragedies that come with travel. They get caught in the rut of daily performing. Or they just don't know how unique an experience they are having.

Not so with Michael Kostroff. Michael's "road virginity" was shattered after many years as a working professional. Having acted in theater and cabaret, television and film—he finally got to realize his dream of traveling in glorious roles throughout the United States. He toured with two major companies in two of Broadway's most successful musicals. And in that time, he experienced the sublime and the ridiculous. But Michael never became oblivious.

In fact, Michael began early on to record the events, emotions, experiences and education of his journey. In a series of deeply felt, profoundly funny, and delightfully human letters to friends, he chronicled his trip with humor and sage insight. The result is the book you have before you.

I'd worked with Michael on a few occasions, but really got to know him when I joined the Los Angeles company of *The Producers*, as Max Bialystock. Michael had already been on tour for several months by then, playing several key roles in the show, as well as understudying mine. I came to adore him both onstage and off.

Letters From Backstage is a gift from a performer to performers and from a traveler to those who love travel. It doesn't matter if you know the shows, or the cities in which he performs them. It is not a particular show or a single town that make these pages worthy. Rather, it is his ability to convey a rich and colorful life with the skill of a seasoned novelist. It doesn't matter that you don't know him. He is still writing to you. You will find yourself in places and situations you know yet have never experienced. You will join his company. And what fine company it is.

So, come . . . tiptoe up onto the stage. Peer into the darkness; push back the velvet curtain, and step into that magical, mysterious world where the most colorful people on earth work and play. You have an all-access pass. Welcome. Enjoy.

Jason Alexander

PREFACE

AT THE RIPE OLD AGE OF FORTY-ONE, after many years as a successful working actor, my childhood dream came true. I was cast in the first national tour of a Broadway musical. But this is not so much a story about my career, or even about theatre, as much as it is about the experience of life on the road with a show.

Letters from Backstage started as a series of e-mails to friends back home. I wanted to take them all with me, put them in the room, and share the adventure. These e-mails quickly grew into a series of short stories—one from each city. After a while, my coworkers started asking for them—cast members, musicians, stage hands. Then they, in turn, forwarded their favorite chapters to family members, who forwarded them to *their* friends. I had constant requests to add people to the mailing list. Before I knew it, I had a readership that extended far beyond my little circle, and even beyond the show business community.

I've always enjoyed the fact that even those who don't know me seem to take such pleasure in reading these little missives. I've tried to make them as intimate and close-up as possible. As you read, maybe you too will begin to feel like you're out there on the road with us.

These chapters were written for my friends. I hope you will do me the great honor to count yourself among them.

Michael Kostroff

THANK-YOUS

THANKS TO TOM CHILD, my writing mentor, without whom I never would have put fingertip to computer keyboard.

. . . And thanks to Linda Griffin, for inspiring me with her own road journals.

. . . And thanks to Ame Stargensky—my writer buddy—for criticism that's so damned . . . *right* all the time, for pushing me, kicking and screaming, against my will, to be a better writer, and for many, many hours of laughter.

Thanks to Sharon Bordas, for urging me to write a book proposal. In fact, thanks to all of you who felt that *Letters from Backstage* would look good in print.

Thanks, as always, to my wonderful, supportive circle of friends.

And a very special thank you to everyone involved with *The Producers* and *Les Misérables*, for the adventures of a lifetime.

ACKNOWLEDGEMENTS

WHEN I WAS ON THE ROAD, I was lousy about taking photos, evidenced by the fact that there is *not one* of me as Max Bialystock in *The Producers*. Several people have been particularly generous in helping me compensate for that shortcoming. They are:

Cast members Pamela Bradley, Jennifer Clippinger, Michael Thomas Holmes, Nancy Johnston, and Jessica Sheridan, of *The Producers*, who were kind enough to share their personal photos.

The remarkable Marci Cochran and Robert Krueger (of the Portland Regional Arts & Cultural Council), Barbara Fox (of the Portland Marriott Downtown Waterfront), and Linda Jackson (Dance and Audience Development Manager at Playhouse Square Center in Cleveland), who actually went out and *took* the photos I needed. You've done your cities proud!

I also want to acknowledge my wonderful pal, Patrick Richwood, who contributed the great cartoon you'll find in the middle of the book (no peeking!).

. . . And my unofficial "editors," Mary Barnes, Sharon Bordas, Pierce Brandt, Deb Glancy, Sue Judin, and Ame Stargensky, for their invaluable input.

. . . And of course, my *official* editors, Nicole Potter-Talling and Jessica Rozler, as well as the rest of the talented, wonderfully collaborative team at Allworth Press, for patiently guiding me through my very first literary venture.

PROLOGUE
(OR "HOW I GOT THAT JOB")

When the world-famous musical *Les Misérables* came to Broadway from its successful run in Europe, the creators realized that they needed to make a few changes for the U.S. production. Most significantly, they decided to add a prologue.

You see, in France, audiences were already familiar with the story, because virtually *everyone* there had read the book. (From what I hear, it's not unusual for a French baby's first words to be "mama," "papa," "wine," "Brie," and "Victor Hugo.") They already knew that Jean Valjean, the hero of the piece, is arrested for stealing a loaf of bread, serves nineteen years in prison, and is then released, a bitter convict, into the cruel world of nineteenth-century France. They knew by heart the part of the story where a kindly, devout bishop gives Valjean the silver he'd tried to steal, and charges him to use the money to become an honest man, thereby utterly changing the direction of Jean's life.

So originally, the musical picked up the story at a much later point, after all that stuff had already happened.

But on the whole, Americans aren't quite as familiar with the great, classic novel. So for our benefit, they tacked on a prologue, which barrels through all of the foregoing, allowing us to feel as savvy and well-read as any French baby. And thank God. Without it, we'd all be lost.

Similarly, as I prepare to welcome a whole new group of readers, and share what was once a series of personal letters to friends, I've decided, after the fact, to briefly race you through the journey that led to this particular adventure. This way, when they produce *Letters from Backstage: The Musical, you* can be the snooty, well-read ones.

I was one of those kids who grew up dreaming of being in a Broadway show. When I got old enough, I began to pursue that dream. Everyone's path is different. In my case, I had some personal hurdles to jump before I could present myself confidently, and I never booked a professional, paying stage acting job until I was thirty years old. Then again, I've always been a late bloomer.

As an aspiring actor in New York, I basically never worked. Well, that's not true. I worked. I worked at Houlihan's, Dallas BBQ, Fandango Bistro, Curtain Up, Miss Grimble's Café, Marvin's Place (where the owner told me not to be so friendly, and to cut the limes smaller because they were expensive), and *very* briefly at the Coconut Grill, an establishment from which I was fired because I got "too hyper" when things got busy.

Strange but true: I liked waiting tables. It was a social job. People were out to enjoy themselves, so I encountered them at a time when they were more likely to be in a good mood . . . though not always. And in New York, waiters talk back to their customers. They're *expected* to have personalities. That gave me a chance to subtly practice the dialects and behavioral traits of my patrons, which always seemed to add up to better tips. People like people who remind them of themselves.

But more than that, I liked waiting tables because it has for decades—if not centuries—been the official support job of the aspiring professional actor. With my first recitation of the nightly specials, I felt I had officially joined a sacred order. Balancing plates was a rite of passage. "Now, finally," I thought, "I'm a real actor."

As fulfilling as all that was, believe it or not, I aspired to more. I hoped eventually to become that *other* kind of actor—the kind who gets *acting* work. So, as an experiment, I moved to Los Angeles for six months. That was fourteen years ago, and though it appears I'm still here, I insist: I'm just visiting. I am, forever and always, a New Yorker.

LA turned out to be a good move. Over the years, I managed to build a solid career in television and regional theatre. Eventually, I was able to give up my day job, as they say, and make a living in the arts—something I never imagined possible. So I stayed. And my childhood dream of being in a big Broadway show became one of those things you just let go of as you get older and more realistic about life. It was okay. I was a working actor, and that was more than enough. In our business, working at all is, in itself, an accomplishment.

My chosen profession has caused me to do some very, very strange things. Like walk into a nearly empty room where two or three people sit behind a bare table, hand music to a pianist, stand on a little X and sing, then leave. It's the kind of thing that sounds incredibly silly if you stop and think about it, so we don't. And yet, I've carried out that bizarre sequence over and over again. It's how a musical theatre actor gets a job. It was a very long time before I could audition like this without coming across like a nervous, raving idiot. Now, I actually enjoy it.

I happen to be blessed with a wonderful, dedicated, passionate stage agent, Eric Stevens. Eric loves the theatre as much as he loves making deals for his actors. I had only recently started working with him when he phoned one day and began the conversation with a phrase that, I have come to learn, is Eric's puckish way of letting you know he has something tasty to report: "Now here's something interesting . . . " he began.

"They want to see you for the national tour of *The Producers*. You need to fly to New York. They're sending you right to callbacks. You'll be singing for Mel Brooks and the director, Susan Stroman. They're considering you for the lead role, Max Bialystock. It's the Nathan Lane role."

Thud. I looked at the phone as if it were broken. "You're joking. How did this happen?"

"I'm your agent! That's how!"

And so I began to prepare for the audition, carefully studying the huge packet of scenes and songs I'd received in the mail.

And I started to get nervous. It's a normal reaction. So I pulled myself aside for a little chat. "Okay, Michael. Listen to me," I said. "There is no point in getting nervous, and here's why: You are not going to get this job. Too many talented New York stage actors with Broadway credits. It's not going to happen, so just let it go. But one thing is guaranteed: The legendary Mel Brooks and the celebrated Susan Stroman are both going to take three minutes out of their busy lives to listen to you sing a funny song in an audition studio on Broadway. Now, if you're nervous, you're going to miss out on one of the coolest moments in your life! Don't do that to yourself. Go enjoy it. Be in the room. Relish it!" This became my mantra. And it calmed me right down. I wasn't going to New York to get a job. I was going there to enjoy the wildly unexpected honor of singing for two entertainment legends—maybe even making them laugh!

I was so successful in this mental preparation that, weeks later, as I stood there singing, I remember thinking, "Wow. This really is cool."

I hadn't planned on a second audition. So when they asked me to come back the next day, I had to rearrange my return flight. I was thrilled. Apparently, I hadn't stunk up the room. I'd get to sing a funny song for these folks again. The next day, forty-seven people sat behind the table where Brooks, Stroman, and a few associates had sat the day before. There was tension in the room. I've learned, over time, that it falls to me to break that tension. As I walked to the little *X* in the center of the floor and prepared to sing, two of Ms. Stroman's associates got up from the table and headed for the door. "I don't know what it is," I quipped. "Whenever it's announced that I'm going to be singing, people put on their coats and leave." Everyone laughed gratefully, and Mel Brooks fell out of his chair. I can now die happy.

After I sang my song, they had me read several scenes and put me through some simple dance moves. At moments like this, you try not to notice how well things are going, but the fact is that this much attention is usually a good sign. Finally, they said, "Thank you," which is auditionese for "We're done now."

And I went home and resumed my life.

A month later, Eric called to say, "Now here's something interesting. They want to see you again."

"Again?"

"Yes, they're flying you to New York on their dime and putting you up at the Hotel Pseudonym."

"*The Pseudonym*? That's a swanky place! What is it these people think I can do for them?"

The upscale Hotel Pseudonym was staffed entirely by sneering sexy people in black. I'm pretty sure they send them for some kind of Resentment Training before allowing them to deal with the public. Catering to the less-than-famous wasn't . . . well . . . paramount. The lobby was trendy and candle-lit, and none of the doors had identifying placards. You just had to know which one was the business center and which one was the broom closet. Each elevator was lit with a different color. I liked the orange one best, because I could almost make out the numbers on the buttons. Everything was dark and stark and hip and imposing. My room was microscopic. The room service menu (two sheets of white paper, typed and stapled) gave no further descriptions than "omelet," "bread," "chicken sandwich." Everything said, "We're really far too interesting to care that you're here." This wasn't doing much for my nerves. Why couldn't *The Producers* have been stingy and put me at a friggin' Motel 6? I went to a nearby, cheap, friendly, well-lit coffee shop for dinner, and tried to un-intimidate myself.

The next morning, I returned to the now familiar audition studio. This time, they really put me through the paces. I gave a whole concert, then they had me read a handful of scenes—not only Max's, but other characters' as well. Then they thanked me again. And you all know what that means. So off I went.

Just outside the door, the nerves I'd successfully kept at bay broke through. I was breathing hard and shaking when the casting director came out into the hall to stop me.

"Michael?" (Oh no. Now what?) "I have to ask you something."

"Yes! Sure! Anything! What?" I said. (What could he possibly want? I sang, I danced, I made Mel Brooks laugh . . . what's left?)

"Now look, Michael. I know that you work in television, and I know you're very successful."

"Yes," I said, with a totally straight face.

"Now, look," he continued. "We don't know what we're doing with the lead role yet, and we have to consider all of our options, so I just have to ask you . . . ."

"Yes?" I said, casually leaning against the wall to steady myself.

"We have these character roles in the show, and you'd be understudying the lead role of Max in a *big* way . . . "

And I'm thinking, "Wait a minute. Is this man *pitching The Producers* to me?"

"I just want to ask you: Would you consider that? Or would you only accept the lead?"

My brain spun like a Rolodex. For half a second, I weighed the option of being very cool, and telling him I'd have to think about it. But I just couldn't. The moment was too much of a milestone.

"Here's my answer: I do work a lot in television. But in my heart, I'm a theatre guy. And it would be my dream come true to do *any* role that you'd like to offer me in *The Producers.*"

We had a moment of true connection. He looked in my eyes and smiled. "That's a really good answer." I think he loved the theatre too.

"Well, that's what you can tell everyone in that room," I said, "because it's the truth."

And I flew home again.

The next morning, I called Eric to say I thought I could have done better, and maybe he should tell them that. He laughed. "I'm not going to call them and tell them you didn't think you were very good."

A half hour later he called me back. "By the way, what are you doing for lunch?"

"I already have plans."

"Aw, that's too bad."

"Why?"

"Because you got it."

There was silence.

My voice dropped two octaves: "what?"

And this wonderful agent . . . sniffled! "You did it, baby. You booked *The Producers*. I'm so proud of you. You start on . . . " and he launched into the details. It sounded like Charlie Brown's teacher: "Wah-wa-wa-wa-wah-wah . . . "

"Eric . . . sorry . . . I'm not hearing any of this . . . Can you go back to the other part?"

"You mean the part where I tell you you've been cast in the first national tour of *The Producers*? That part?"

I smiled. "That's the part. Just wanted to make sure I'd heard it. Can you tell me the rest later? Because nothing else is coming through."

The months that followed are a blur now, but I know I sublet my apartment, bought a new suitcase, and told all my friends. I also had a prior commitment to do *A Funny Thing Happened on the Way to the Forum* in Utah, which would close, conveniently, about a week before rehearsals would start for *The Producers*, giving me time to get settled in New York, and with any luck, compose myself. At the moment, composing myself seemed like a pretty unrealistic goal. I was on the ceiling.

And that's how it all started. Not exactly Victor Hugo, but then, he never balanced four plates on his arm, so there.

Happy reading,
Kostroff

1
JE SUIS ARRIVÉ!
(... GIVE OR TAKE)

July 15th, 2002

Hello, friends,

Well, I'm here.

Yesterday, I bid farewell to Ogden, Utah (having closed my fourth production of *A Funny Thing Happened on the Way to the Forum*), and hello to New York City, my hometown, where, in just over a week, I'll start rehearsals for the first national tour of *The Producers!*

Well . . . to be more accurate, I said hello to a city called West New York, New Jersey, which I never even knew existed. My home for the next two weeks is my friend Stephanie's place, just a stone's throw from midtown Manhattan, with a view of the skyline to plotz from. After that, I'll move into the city itself, where Jeff and Chris, two guys I don't even know, have generously invited me to stay for the rest of the rehearsal period, simply by virtue of a mutual friendship. Outrageously kind of them.

I love my city. And I've really missed it. Hardly slept last night. Just sat there looking at it, across the water, like a photo of a lover.

There's something about your hometown, wherever it is. It just smells right. The water tastes right. The sounds at night–in this case air conditioners, groaning bus brakes, and screaming ambulances—are comforting. They're what you remember night sounds to be.

So here I am, in a kind of giddy limbo: right on the brink of something I dreamed of all my life. Knowing it's starting in just over a week . . . but not yet. Not yet. Totally loopy from lack of sleep—only a couple of hours last night, and the night before, I helped strike the set in Utah until 3 AM, so I'm shot. And idiotically happy. Hard to believe I'm home . . . nearly, and about to begin what will surely be an extraordinary next chapter of my life.

This week's agenda is as follows: I've been asked by *The Producers'* stage manager whether I could possibly make time to see the Broadway show. Well, sure, it's a terrible burden, attending Broadway's biggest hit in decades, but hey—I'm a team player. It's sold out, of course, but as a *cast member* (can you stand it?), I get to knock on the stage door, tell them I'm with the national tour, and watch from the steps that lead to the balcony. Forget it, I'm beside myself. To me, that's better than any seat in the house. It's so good it's ridiculous. So that's Tuesday. On Wednesday I take the *train*, if you please (a very theatrical mode of transportation) to Baltimore, where I'll be shoot-ing an episode of *The Wire*, the HBO series on which I have a recurring role as a horrible shark of an attorney who defends drug dealers. (Really great show, and a terrific role.) Then on Friday, it's back here, where I'll see old friends, wander the city, and try to pull myself together for my first rehearsal the following Monday; that's when the real adventure begins.

For now, I'm in limbo, in a city that's not quite New York and barely New Jersey, just waiting. The anticipation is electric. Still, I hope I can relax enough to sleep sometime between now and then. I can't show up to meet Susan Stroman and Mel Brooks with bags under my eyes.

Sit tight for updates.
Kostroff

2
BROADWAY BOOT CAMP

September 7th, 2002

Hey, friends,

The past seven weeks—from my first rehearsal for *The Producers* to today, my last day in New York before going on the road—have been, as you can well imagine, quite an adventure. I expected to be able to bring you all up to date before now, but my brain has been too full and my body too tired to even think about putting it all into words. But now, as I pack my suitcases and prepare to embark on the tour for which we've been rehearsing, I have, finally, the time and the perspective to assess a bit. And there's a lot to tell. So here, then, is my overdue . . . and overstuffed . . . report.

When I last wrote to you all, I was gazing at Manhattan from my window in New Jersey, unable to sleep from the excitement—the excitement of being back home, and the even greater excitement of being in the national tour of a Broadway show. I didn't know then that it would be the last time I'd have any trouble sleeping at all.

Back then, in the good old days before the craziness began, I was in a dreamy state of disbelief. But as of the first rehearsal, there was a sharp and immediate shift in my state of mind. Because suddenly, as with any show, there was *work* to do—lines and blocking and dance steps and harmonies to learn. Lots and lots of them. No time to be goofy and blissful–I was busy! So, while still excited, I found myself in a solid, clear, highly focused, professional mode.

The first thing that was markedly and refreshingly different from previous theatre experiences was that here, every person in every department was on his gig. And I mean *on* it! Things were organized and scheduled and correct down to the very last detail, thanks in large part to our superb stage manager, Rolt. (If you know me, you know how I relish accuracy and efficiency, so naturally, I was his instant fan.) We had information packets. We had rehearsal mock-ups of props and costumes. Everything happened on time. And everything had been carefully thought through in advance: At our first music rehearsal, I was amazed to find that the musical director remembered our voices from the auditions, and had already worked out who'd sing which parts. None of the usual hunting and pecking. Rather, "Now here in bar 126, where the baritones split into two parts, Michael, you're on the F. Patrick, you take the A flat."

During the first week, the ensemble rehearsed without the leads, so we could get a head start on the big numbers. I was shocked by how much dancing my track* involved. Dancing, folks. Real dancing: turns, jumps . . . stuff with French names. Now, I'm forty-one, and not exactly in Olympic shape. Actors of my type–character actors–aren't usually asked to do a lot of dancing. In fact, most choreographers are pleasantly surprised if we have any sense of rhythm at all. But in a Susan Stroman show, everybody dances. Everybody. And since the show had already been done on Broadway, it was all set. It wasn't as if they were going to tailor the steps to our abilities, or lack thereof. So we did it. There were several moments when I remember thinking, "Well, clearly, I'm going to be fired. I can't possibly do what

---

* *track: Musical theatre term meaning the sequence of roles played by a single ensemble member during the course of a performance. Since ensemble members often make several appearances within the same show, this term is used rather than "part" or "role," which would indicate a single character.*

they're showing me." (P. S. Now I do those same steps at every run-through like it's nothing. I even have tap shoes. Tap shoes, ladies and gentlemen. More on that later.)

(And I weigh 142 pounds.)

(Okay, I'm lying about that last part.)

The folks in charge were friendly and warm, but there wasn't a moment wasted, and we worked very quickly. By the end of the first day, we'd learned vocal parts and choreography for the first two numbers. By the end of the second day, we'd polished those numbers and added a few more. By the end of the third day, my thighs were on fire. My knees ached. The soles of my feet wept with every step on the way home as I wondered why anyone would want to go into this stupid business anyway.

On Thursday, after singing and dancing all day, I stepped into New York's sweltering heat and walked to Penn Station, where I once again boarded a train bound for Baltimore to film yet another episode of *The Wire*. In Baltimore, I shot till 4:30 AM, grabbed what could only be called a nap at the hotel there, then took the train back to New York, where I arrived just in time for the Friday morning rehearsal. I did the same thing the next night and twice the following week, getting myself very sick, but impressing everyone. Yeah, I was exhausted, and sick, and every muscle ached, but even still, I couldn't help feeling ridiculously cheerful. I mean really . . . how do you complain? An HBO series and a national tour of Broadway's biggest hit. Boo fuckin' hoo.

At the beginning of the second week, we had a huge meet-and-greet at the rehearsal studio. Anyone with even the remotest connection was invited. Mel Brooks was there, along with all the creators, producers, designers, people who book the tour, casting folks, assistant assistants, the guy who hangs the posters, the lady who typed the script, the man who invented music—everybody who was anybody and even some who weren't. Seated in folding chairs, we did a read-through of the show. There was lots of laughter and bagels and hugging. It was *very* exciting. Mel Brooks kissed me on the cheek like an uncle and said, "We didn't think you'd do this!

You're so good!" Mel Brooks, you understand. THE Mel Brooks. I almost choked on my rugalach.

And then everyone left, and it was back to work. Susan Stroman, like most director/choreographers, is very specific about movement. Scenes are blocked like dances, so there's a lot to learn. It's a very different way of working from what most of us are used to. Normally, for example, we'd be directed to "enter when you hear this cue line." But here, it was broken down into the precise syllables of the cue line and the specific foot on which you land as you enter. I guess by now we'd all figured out that the goal was for us to do exactly what was done by the original Broadway cast— down to gestures and line readings. And to be very honest, that was tough for most of us, because sometimes, what's funny on one person falls flat when someone else attempts it. Thankfully, Ms. Stroman and her expert team are really good at explaining the ideas *behind* the gestures, so we don't feel quite so robotic, and that's a blessing. They're also very encouraging. They seem sincerely pleased with this cast.

Still, week three was the one during which each of us, privately and unbeknownst to each other, went secretly psycho. As we tried our best to give the production team exactly what they wanted, all our worst stuff started to haunt us. We got paranoid and neurotic and insecure and generally mental. As for yours truly, I got it in my mind that I'd said the wrong thing to everyone and asked too many questions and now, as a result, no one could stand me. Rational, right? I learned later, to my great relief, that I wasn't the only one, as fellow cast members confessed privately, "Man! Last week I thought they were thinking they'd made a big mistake hiring me!" Really, it was just exhaustion. We were all sore and tired and we had, by then, so much choreography and so many gestures and movements to remember that our brains were bursting. So we all got a little crazy. Fortunately, I was smart enough to keep my dark imaginings to myself, tempted though I was to apologize to everyone for each fictional faux pas.

By now, we were staging the famous "Springtime for Hitler" number— a *fantastically* busy, funny, and brilliantly choreographed piece during which everyone keeps changing costumes and coming back as other people. The associate choreographer jumped from dancer to dancer, demonstrating each one's individual steps, then leaving him to practice as he moved on to the next one. "Okay," he said when he got to me. "And it's hop-shuffle-ball-change-step-step." I turned white as a sheet.

"Umm . . . tap dancing?"

"Yes, Michael. This is tap dancing. So: hop-shuffle—"

"Umm . . . I don't tap," I confessed sheepishly. "I'm sorry. You never asked at the audition."

"Uh-huh," he replied casually, as if I'd said something about the weather. "So: hop-shuffle-ball-change—"

"I'm not going to have to actually make the sounds, am I?"

"Yes, Michael. You'll be wearing tap shoes, and that's what they're for. Just watch me: hop-shuffle-ball-change-step-step." He wouldn't take no for an answer, and wasn't the least bit thrown by the fact that I'd never tapped a step in my life. I don't know. There's something magical about this approach. They assume you can do it, and it's bloody contagious. I gave it a shot. I was lousy, but determined

Hop-shuffle-ball change-step-step. Yaka-daka-dak dak dak. Every day, whenever there was a break, I'd practice. "Yaka-dak—oh, damn it!" "Yaka-daka-dak—*crap*!" The expert tappers in the cast gave pointers:

"Do it like your foot is drunk."

"Keep your weight even."

"Lay into the shuffle more."

"Think about something else."

My tap dancing still stunk, but now I had *techniques*. Okay . . . I was improving. A little.

I was asked, officially, to understudy the lead, which was a tremendous honor. And a few days later, Ms. Stroman pulled me aside and asked if I'd also understudy an additional role, Roger De Bris (originated by the great Gary Beach). She seemed to think I could handle the additional responsibility. I was flattered, but skeptical. "*Really*??" I asked incredulously. "Are you *sure?*"—forgetting that I was questioning a Tony Award–winning director!

"You'll be fine," she said. And I believed her.

Every night after rehearsal, I'd regale my hosts, Jeff and Chris, with the latest play-by-play, demonstrating my newest dance steps and sharing all the dish. It's hard to believe I didn't know these guys when the process started. I'm crazy about them!

Slowly, the show started to get into my body. Some nights, I even found the energy to go to dinner with New York friends. And members of the company relaxed enough to start noticing each other's work. We have a terrific cast, led by Lewis J. Stadlen and Don Stephenson, who, it's my guess, are going to be the best guys yet to play these roles. Naturally, I'm biased. The supporting players are hilarious. And our ensemble is like a singing, dancing, comedic SWAT team—lean and mean—a cast of thousands played by just sixteen of us. Then there are the swings*—an amazing group of seasoned pros who seem to be able to do anything that's thrown at them.

My particular track is fairly nonstop, and I like it that way. In addition to all the group numbers, I'll be playing Mr. Marks, a sadistic CPA who terror-izes his employees; Kevin, a ridiculously swishy costume designer; Jack Lepidus, an *awful* tenor auditioning for the role of Hitler; and the Judge, who sends our heroes to prison. In between, I play everything from a newspaper man to a Bavarian peasant to a dancing prisoner. This, my friends, is a really great job.

During week four, we had a run-through of the entire show, top to bottom, for an audience of invited guests that included friends, the casting people, and the Broadway company of the show. Nervous? Oh hell yes. These were the first "outsiders" to see our production, so although we were

---

* *swings: Cast members who are not in the regular performing cast, but who travel with the company, to cover any absences in the ensemble. Swings are each required to know multiple tracks, so that they can step in—sometimes at a moment's notice—as needed! In our show, swings cover leads as well, for a minimum of six tracks each!*

still at the studio, in rehearsal clothes, we wanted to really show them something. They couldn't have been a better audience. They screamed and hooted and clapped when we entered the room, laughed at all the jokes (even though they knew them), and

At work in the rehearsal studio.

applauded for what felt like ten minutes after each number. I botched my tap step and my fan kick, but they were a forgiving group, and didn't seem to notice. Afterwards, we got to meet a bit. I thanked one of the Broadway guys for showing up at 10:30 AM—a painfully early hour for show folks. "Are you kidding?" he said, "We couldn't wait! Don't forget, we've never gotten to see this thing! We're *in* it!"

Whenever I'd pass the associate choreographer in a hallway, he'd test me on my tap step: yaka-daka-dak dak—*feces*!! I seemed to do it worse when he was watching. Ugh. My albatross.

At the end of four weeks, the entire company began busing to Newark, New Jersey, for technical rehearsals at a huge theatre there, the New Jersey Performing Arts Center. The crew had set up the entire show: sets, costumes, lighting, sound—we had everything except the orchestra, who'll join us in Pittsburgh.

The onstage singing and dancing, as impressive as they are, are nothing compared to the "backstage ballet," as I call it. I have (I believe I counted them correctly) *fourteen* costume changes—*four* of them within "Springtime for Hitler"! At one point, I get completely dressed in a full tux, hat, gloves, and overcoat just to walk out from the wings and through an onstage door. You can't imagine the scene back there. It's this insane yet well-choreographed mish-mash of flying clothes and actors and wigs and dressers and set pieces and props, all narrowly missing each other and yet, all contributing to the clean, tight show the audience is seeing onstage. You'd never know the madness behind the slickness. Really, we should sell tickets!

Working all this out took some doing. It was tiring and intense, but enormously fun, especially as we began having run-throughs for invited audiences. Now we were in a theatre, with the set and all the technical elements. It was starting to feel like a show. The audience went nuts, and we all remembered what a funny and entertaining musical *The Producers* is!

By now I was nailing my tap step nearly every time: Yaka-daka-dak dak dak. Yaka-daka-dak dak dak. Look, ma'. I'm dancin'! I ran into the associate choreographer in the hallway. I knew he'd noticed, and that a big compliment was coming my way. He gave me the warmest, widest grin, nodded approvingly, patted my arm, and said sweetly, "It could be a bit louder."

Toward the end of these tech rehearsals, I began to get back some of that fizzy feeling about going on the road. I'd lost it for a while, buried as I was in THE WORK—the vast amount of new information being assimilated by my body and brain. But as I began to "own" my track a tiny bit, and as our Pittsburgh packets were handed out, with maps, schedules, and our first plane tickets . . . I felt I was finally beginning, for the first time, to truly grasp what was happening: My lifelong dream of being an itinerant stage actor in a big Broadway musical was coming true.

For the past two days, while our set and lights travel to Pittsburgh, a small group of us have been back in the studio for understudy rehearsals. While most of the cast enjoyed much-needed days off, we gathered to work on the roles we cover. It was a nice, quiet, low-key time after all the running around—kind of like being a summer camp counselor who's just put the last kid on the bus back home. I was taught all of Max's blocking and choreography by the associate director/choreographer. It was so helpful to run the scenes and songs on my feet. Still, I'm hoping not to go on as Max too soon.

Today, I rested, packed, and reminisced for the first time since my arrival in New York. It's been a soupy whirlpool. A roller coaster ride. Exhausting, funny, educational, difficult, demanding, fulfilling . . . and the tour hasn't even started yet!

Tomorrow . . . we fly to Pittsburgh. Yaka-daka-dak dak dak!

Kostroff

3

FIRST OF ALL, PITTSBURGH

September 18th, 2002

Dear friends,

Pittsburgh has been a city of firsts: The first stop of our tour, our first hotel, our first paying audiences, and in just a few hours, our first opening night. There will be many more of them to come as we weave our way across the country. But of course, this is the big one, since it launches the tour.

Some of our firsts have been unexpected ones. During understudy rehearsals in New York, the covers* for the role of Ulla were going over a particularly tricky dance sequence—one that contains what I've labeled The Forbidden Step, since Ullas keep getting injured doing it. And that's exactly what happened. Two of them got hurt at the same instant. One of them, Jennifer, was hurt badly enough that she had to go to the hospital. She showed up for our first flight in a cast. But Melissa (one of our crackerjack swings) stepped in, and has been doing a flawless job. Jennifer hates to miss opening night, but is wisely taking the time to heal. Thus, we've had our company's first injury, and Melissa's first performance.

The Benedum Center—our first theatre—is gorgeous. A huge, old, ornate palace with enough backstage space for a whole other show! It's moving to

---

* *covers: Understudies.*

think that someone loved theatre enough to build such a place. Outside: our first marquee!

The preview audiences have been *loving* the show. It's something heady to look out from the stage and see them piled all the way up to the top balcony,

The Benedum Center, September 2002.

which seems miles in the air, and hear them laughing. They seem so happy to be there. There have been nightly standing ovations for our stars. It's pretty damned cool.

You'll also be proud to know, dear readers, that yours truly has the distinction of being responsible for the first ad-lib of the tour. Toward the end of the show, Max is in jail, awaiting trial. He sings "Betrayed." After the song, his jail cell splits in two and goes off into the wings as a backdrop rises, revealing a courtroom. I play the judge.

One night, the backdrop rose, but only half of the jail cell went off. The other half stayed onstage, stuck in the track on which it travels. (We're in previews. These things happen.) After an awkward pause, a stagehand came on and pushed the set piece off into the wings. In character as the judge, I just shook my head and muttered, "We have more trouble with those things." The audience laughed and applauded, and my fellow performers nearly broke, which was even better.

In the midst of all these previews there were continuing daily rehearsals, which made for quite a tiring week. I began to notice that most of the rehearsals were centered around me learning the lead role of Max. And then the associate director casually mentioned one afternoon that if Lew Stadlen goes out, I'll be the first cover to go on. (There are two Max understudies: Fred Applegate and me. Fred is *brilliant* as Franz Liebkind, the Nazi playwright, so I imagine they're reluctant to move him out of that role to play Max.) And that was the other surprise first of the week: first cover. If Stadlen is out, I'm the guy. I'm it. I'm the star. I got a little queasy at the thought.

No. I got a lot queasy.

Now, I'm not being coy. I realize it sounds glamorous. But I want you to really think about it: Think about suddenly leading a big fat Tony Award–winning Broadway show. Think about putting on the costume—an exact replica of the one worn by the famous Nathan Lane. Think about stepping onto the stage in front of thousands of people and saying the star's lines. If that still sounds like lighthearted fun to you, you're not really picturing it yet, because it's *damned scary*. Honestly, who'd want to do this?

Lew, meanwhile, had been working nonstop—between rehearsals and performances—and I marveled that he was still standing, let alone singing and dancing. (It's a bitch of a role, for those of you who haven't seen the show.) I realized I could go on at any moment. Holy shit. This isn't happening.

That night, I had this nightmare. I was being chased all over creation by someone who wanted to kill me. (I don't know why. Don't bother me with details when my life is in peril.) I ran and ran, seeking out the most obscure hiding places I could find. But escape was nearly impossible because, darn the luck, my stalker had psychic powers, and could find me wherever I went . . . not unlike a stage manager, who can find you wherever you are to let you know you're going on that night. I didn't need a dream book to figure that one out. I was so terrified by the prospect of playing Max that it felt like someone was trying to kill me.

Since then I've gotten *slightly* calmer about the whole thing. But I must say I get a big smile on my face every time I arrive at the theatre and see Lew there.

Moments ago, in the midst of writing this, I got a call summoning me to an emergency put-in rehearsal for Kevin, who understudies the role of

Roger De Bris, the deliciously bad, flamboyontly gay director of *Springtime for Hitler.* The excitement never ends. Looks like Kevin may be going on tonight—opening night! Another first! Better him than me.

So I gotta go rehearse. And then, I'll press my fancy-schmantzy outfit for

Rolt, our stage manager . . . lurking in the backstage darkness. Photo: Michael Thomas Holmes.

tonight's party, and get ready to wow our first group of theatre critics! I'll keep you all posted. And if anything newsworthy happens . . . you'll be the first to know.

Kostroff

4

THE DARK MYSTERIES
OF CLEVELAND

October 19th, 2002

Hello again, friends,

I believe it was Ralph Waldo Emerson who wrote, "Cleveland sucks . . . and I'm not kidding, either." Boy, that guy had a way with words. And our company of *The Producers* would probably agree unanimously. But for us, the suckiness of Cleveland has come in the form of such a strange variety of coincidences that we decided, just for our own amusement, to blame some mystical condition pervading the city.

Okay . . . it's not all bad. Our apartments at the City Court are nice. It's a great change to have a kitchen and a living room after being in a hotel for a month. (I've never been so thrilled to toast a bagel.) And there's a laundry room, a grocery store, a coffee place, a pool, and a bar—all right there in the building. All truly fantastic . . . especially the bar. And hey, we're employed!

But almost since our arrival, we've been plagued by what we've come to call "Clevelanditis," an affliction of the psyche that makes one moody, melancholy, strange, susceptible to cold and flu, and generally blechy.

There seems to be a cloud of dreariness over the whole place, and with remarkable uniformity, everyone feels it.

So come with me now, brave traveler, through this city of dark exotic mysteries, with its mind-bending twists and turns . . . its eerie atmosphere that bewitches the unwitting visitor. Question all you know as you make your way along these winding streets, full of shifting perceptions and ancient curses. Follow closely, friend, or lose your soul . . . We're in Cleveland.

The moment I arrived, my computer stopped working. Two hours earlier, in Pittsburgh, it had been fine. Now, the screen was blank. It was an omen.

The next day, we were called early to the theatre to work things out in the new space. We arrived to find bedlam, as the load-in of the sets and lighting was running late. It seemed impossible that we'd be ready for our show that night.

Now as a sidebar, here's something I found astonishing about the way things work as we transition from city to city: We do a closing Sunday night show. The curtain comes down, and the crew immediately starts packing up the sets, costumes, wigs, lighting equipment, stage floor (we travel with our own "deck"), and all the mechanics—a *huge* amount of stuff—into ten trucks, which take off for the next city. Upon arrival, they start setting it all up again. *That following Tuesday night*—just two days later— we open the show in a new city for a paying audience with (are you ready?) a new orchestra, new dressers, and several new crew members. Miraculously, we pull it off!

So, naturally, there's some awkwardness as we adjust to each new theatre. And that was exactly where the real trouble started. The backstage area in Cleveland was tiny compared with Pittsburgh, so we had to squeeze. That first night, everyone was in everyone else's way. Crew members carried set pieces through quick-change areas. Actors ran around loudly whispering in search of their props. People hugged the wall to let others run by to make entrances. It was a Marx Brothers movie. Without the laughs.

As for me, my biggest challenge was working out my quick changes with my new dresser, a lovely older man who was so anxious to help with everything that if I went to take off my hat, he'd "assist" me with it (rather than working on another garment to speed things up) and we'd find ourselves wrestling for control. He'd hand me my pants. I'd take them. He wouldn't let go. I'd go to toss a shirt into the discard bin. He'd intercept and we'd end up throwing it together. Folks, it was the oddest thing. Ever try putting on a tie with four hands? And it went on like this for several nights. We just kept getting in each other's way. Eventually we worked it all out, and fortunately, I've managed to make every entrance.

While the stage floor was tight, the rest of the building was a vast, rambling maze. To get to our dressing rooms we had to go downstairs, past the orchestra pit, around a winding hallway, down a corridor, across state lines, and to the left. Keep in mind, we go back and forth a lot during the show. So every time a number ended, the entire ensemble had to hike, sweaty and panting, back down to the distant catacombs, only to change costumes and repeat the journey back up to the stage. Many joked that we wouldn't need transportation to our next stop, Cincinnati, since that's where the dressing rooms were.

The poor crew, meanwhile, was exhausted from the difficult load-in and little—if any—sleep. The wardrobe people had their hands full finding spots to place the quick-change racks. Things were so tight that our stage manager was stationed way off in a corner, behind huge stacks of equipment, where he could only see the stage on the tiny screen of his black-and-white monitor. I vaguely remember what the guy looks like.

And then, rather ungracefully, the weather changed. Suddenly, it was chilly, windy, rainy, and grey. Fall had arrived, unannounced. We scrambled for our parkas and sweaters.

A nasty little flu, meanwhile, had apparently been alerted to our arrival, and wasted no time in capitalizing on the weather change and working its way through the cast. Jeff, who plays the role of Carmen Ghia, actually went out for several days, and even still looks a bit grey. I narrowly missed the dreaded drek myself, fighting back with ginger, Echinacea, vitamins, water, garlic, voodoo, positive thinking, and anything else I could get my hands on. (Being on "MaxWatch 2002," I have to be extra careful. If our star goes out, I have to be able to go on, and he's fighting the same illness as we speak. It's like being the vice president, or the runner-up Miss America.)

And then there was the neighborhood. Dark. Bleak. Desolate. There's one building on the way to the theatre that we're *sure* is a crack house. After several company members expressed concerns, and one was nearly mugged, a police officer was posted on the corner to make sure we all got home safely at night after the show. It takes a lot to unnerve New Yorkers, but those two blocks did it. Swell town.

All of this made for a few snippy moments among the show folk, and I must confess I had more than my share of them, and had to do a bit of apologizing later. It just sneaked up on me. My muscles hurt. I was tired. I hated Cleveland. And the three-day hike to and from the stage was getting to me.

It took a few days for me to figure it out. Friends, I had crossed over to my dark side. I was bitter, unreasonable, unpleasant, irritable, and . . . ugh, it's so hard to say it . . . I didn't like my job. That's right. A day I never thought would come. And I was furious with myself for that. I thought, "I am *not* this guy! I'm the guy who's always grateful to make a living in the arts! I'm the guy who loves the theatre . . . who's living his lifelong dream come true! I'm in *The Producers*, for Pete's sake!" Nonetheless, this bad attitude persisted for the better part of a week, until it just became funny. Fellow company members would give me a knowing smile and say, "Any better today?"

"I'm gettin' through it," I'd smile back. "What can I tell you?" But inside, I was my own evil twin.

Even in the midst of this, it was hard to take myself too seriously. You can't imagine how ridiculous it is to see a depressed guy in a lace granny dress with black pantyhose, or a Bavarian peasant costume, complete with lederhosen. Even I had to laugh at myself. Still, I was living for Monday, our day off. I figured that would help turn me around.

Finally, Monday came—a chance to rest, restore, and regroup. I got a massage from a masseuse who'd been recommended by the local theatre. Weird and creepy. That's a whole other story in itself. Let it suffice to say that 1) massage was definitely not his forte, 2) I believe he may have been offering other services, and 3) when he left, I was tenser than when he arrived. My shoulders were up near my ears, and I felt greatly in need of a shower.

The bar downstairs, meanwhile, had quite suddenly gone out of business. Something about unpaid rent. Just our luck. If ever we needed a drink . . .

Liza (one of our stage managers), Kevin, and I went to Cleveland's Rock and Roll Hall of Fame for a bit of diversion. "Y'all," announced Kevin (he's from Texas), "this guy told me there's a *great* restaurant on the fourth floor." So up we went, mouths watering, toward the culinary Mecca, visions of something flambé dancing in our heads.

It was a snack bar.

And as we dined on limp club sandwiches, stale potato chips, and rancid coffee, we started to chuckle. Then we started to laugh. Then we started to laugh uncontrollably. Fuckin' Cleveland. We toasted to the man who'd recommended the restaurant, bussed our trays, and went off to see Bobby Sherman's first jumpsuit.

Somehow, after that, I was fine.

I returned to work the next week bearing a remarkable resemblance to an actual human being, as did everyone else. We started having fun again. And the audiences—once the reviews came out—loved the show. I was back to myself, in spite of Cleveland. And thank God for that, because . . .

This morning, as I was editing this chapter, the call came. You know the call I mean.

"Hello?"

"Hey, Michael, this is Rolt."

"Hey, Rolt. Is this the call?"

"This is the call. Lewie's out sick. You're playing Max for the matinee."

"Okay."

I hung up the phone and took a very deep breath. My first reflex was terror. But then, as we all do when stakes are high, I got *extremely* focused. And to my surprise, I realized I wasn't all that nervous. I know it sounds strange. But since going on the road, I'd had meticulous weekly rehearsals in preparation for this very moment. (With audience members paying top dollar for tickets, these Broadway shows don't leave things to chance. They make damned sure the understudy is ready to go on, just in case.) I was ready. And there was something else . . .

Years ago, just as I was starting rehearsals for my first production of *A Funny Thing Happened on the Way to the Forum*, I was suddenly thrust, through some unusual circumstances, into the lead role. The character is hardly ever offstage, and I had eight days to learn the part. I called a friend back in LA in a panic. "All right," she said calmly, "I know you're nervous, but I'm going to tell you something critically important: You *must not* show it. Always remember: *Leading actors must lead.*" A light bulb switched on. I understood. No matter what, even if I was a complete mess, I had to present a composed façade for the rest of the cast so *they* wouldn't be nervous. As the new lead, I had to be the daddy. I had to take care of *them.*

And so, as I walked with determination toward the theatre, I had a mission: Reassure the cast. Let them know we still had a show.

I didn't bother doing a last-minute cram. There were too damned many lines for that. I had to trust that I knew them.

"Oh my God! Michael! I just heard! Are you nervous?" chirped one of our chorus girls as I made my way to the star dressing room for the first time.

"Nah. It'll be fun. How're *you* doing?"

I didn't freak out. Didn't have that luxury. This was the big time, now. I had to deliver. People came to see *The Producers*, and damn it, they were going to get *The Producers*. No matter what, this show was not going to fall apart on my watch.

Jaki is Lew's dresser. She's called the star dresser, for obvious reasons, and she's one of only two dressers who travel with the show. Jaki's a real character—a tough little broad with a heavy Scottish accent, the colorful vocabulary of a truck driver, and a deliciously wicked sense of humor. I once saw this stumpy little fireplug get on the elevator with six of our tall, gorgeous, leggy showgirls. "Out o' me way, ya' fat cows," she barked, and they all shrieked with laughter. I got to the dressing room to find Jaki pressing my Max costume for the first time. "Hey," she nodded calmly, like we did this every day. "You want to go over the fast changes?"

Fast changes? Ugh. It was all I could do to remember the lines and blocking. "Actually, Jaki, if it's up to me, I'd much rather have you just push me around and tell me what to put on and take off."

A sideways grin made its way along her lips. "I c'n do that."

Shortly before the show, Lew's costar, Don Stephenson (he plays Leo Bloom, the role originated by Matthew Broderick), came into the dressing room to check on me. Don is famously reclusive, and we'd barely spoken up till then. But in a few minutes, we'd be sharing the stage. He had my full attention. "I only have one piece of advice for you, Kostroff," he said. "Don't shoot your wad at the matinee. You'll probably be on again tonight. Save something for the second show. See you out there." And with that, he was gone. That was Don's way of saying, "I'm not worried about you. Break a leg."

Well, I wish I had some outrageous story to tell you about playing Max for the first time. But the fact is, I don't remember much. It was a bit of a blur. I *think* I was relatively together, considering the task. All those rehearsals and preparations, and the *fantastic* support from everyone—the cast, stage managers, local crew members, and especially Jaki, my rock, who was there every time I left the stage, pushing me around: "Take off your vest. Put on this tie. Give me your hat. Drink some water. Hurry up, ya' lazy bastard"—kept me loose, and enabled me to get through it with a minimal number of mistakes. In fact, despite the enormity of the role, I had fun! The whole thing felt like a long, crazy ride at Disneyland. Mind you, I was too busy concentrating on the task at hand—three hours' worth of lines, blocking, entrances, exits, choreography, song lyrics, and costume changes—to take in the fact that I was *starring* in the first national tour of *The Producers* that afternoon.

But I must tell you—I need you to know—that this cast was so sweet to me today—supportive, excited, and very kind. When the curtain came down at the end of Act One, they all whooped and shouted and hugged me, and did the same at the end of Act Two. Really, a great group of folks. In the middle of singing the huge eleven o'clock number, "Betrayed"—a long, impossibly energetic solo in which Max recaps the entire show—I glanced into the wings, and saw what looked like the entire cast squeezed together, watching. Like little bats' eyes in a cave. I don't know how many of you are familiar with the score, but this song is a mother. So when I made it successfully to the end, there arose such a cry from the wings, I thought Apaches were attacking on horseback.

When the show was over, I felt like I was made of water. Nothing left. I drifted back to the dressing room. The associate director came in with six pages of notes for me, which I couldn't really take in. I was like an overcooked noodle, just draped into a chair. But I felt wonderful. I was just glad to have gotten through it. Then there was a knock at the door. Fred—the other Max understudy—poked his head in. "Damn you," he said. "Now I'll never get to go on." And he grinned at me widely. "They should give you fifty pages of notes. And every one of them should say 'Thank you.'" And he left.

And then it was just me and Jaki, who was quietly hanging up my costumes. "Wow," I said. "That was wild. I think I did okay."

And this tough little cookie, who's been in the business for years, who has dressed and undressed superstars, and who is fazed by nothing, turned around and said, simply and sincerely, "Kostroff . . . ah' cried." And coming from her, that may have been the dearest comment of all.

I oozed back to my apartment to grab a bite. Rolt phoned to say that I'd be on again for the evening performance. "No worries," I murmured weakly, a little worried. Thank the Lord I'd heeded Don Stephenson's advice and saved something for that second show, though I was thoroughly spent by the time it was over.

It was a great day. And there aren't a lot of those in Cleveland.

Tomorrow's our closing night here. We can hardly wait to shake the dust from our feet and put this city behind us. Monday, we travel. Then, on Tuesday, we open in Cincinnati, in another new space, with another new orchestra, new dressers, and new crew members. Cincinnati has one major thing going for it:

It isn't Cleveland.

More to come . . .

Kostroff

5

"HONEY, THEY'RE SHOWBIRDS."

November 4th, 2002

Dear readers,

The fog has lifted, and the sun has risen again. The people are happy.
There's joy in the village. Chapel bells are ringing! There's cheering, ticker-
tape parades, and dancing in the streets! The evil giant is dead. We have
survived Cleveland, and put it well behind us.

There were no tearful good-byes or last, longing gazes. In fact, when
the final curtain came down on closing night, we all kicked it and gave it
the finger. Good riddance.

And then came Cincinnati, a surprisingly charming city. Of
course, after Cleveland, anyplace else was the friggin' French Riviera as
far as we were concerned. I've never seen such a large group have such
a uniform reaction. Something shifted. Everyone, company-wide,
seemed lighter and happier. People lifted their heads and looked at each
other again. I ran into one of our traveling crew members, Kent,
backstage and asked how he was doing. He shook his head with
relief and said, "Oh, man. *So* much better." Nice to see us all smiling
again.

Two of our leads and one of our many producers are from here, so there have been lots of family and fans at the show, and lots of dinners to attend. Oh, how we suffer.

To me, the coolest thing of all is that you can walk over a bridge and be in Kentucky. Being feeble-witted and easily amused, I walked back and forth over that bridge several times during my stay, just because I got such a kick out of changing states. I even called friends on my cell phone. "I'm in Ohio . . . wait . . . wait . . . wait . . . *now* I'm in Kentucky!" Okay, so I'm an idiot. But in my defense, we're all pretty goofy these days.

Outside our hotel, there's a beautiful walkway with trees and little lights that goes on for several blocks. A great place for walking and thinking. And it's been raining, which I love. One day I took the shuttle over to Kentucky by myself to go to the movie theatre there—rated #1 in the country for first-run movies. Then I took myself out for a terrific lunch at this Tuscan restaurant. (When I told a friend, he said, "I thought all they had in Kentucky was barbecue." Au contraire, mon ami!) I sat there, eating this gorgeous food, sipping hot coffee, with rain falling on the skylight in the ceiling, and I thought, "Holy shit! Who has this life?? This is really good!" And I thought about the terrible darkness of my childhood, and about the romantic disappointments and dire financial tensions of my twenties, and the discouraging career struggles of my thirties, and how impossible it would have been to predict ever being quite this content. I promise not to wax maudlin about my past here, dear readers, but this sweet little moment, at a restaurant in Kentucky, was made even sweeter by how far I had to journey to get here. Far further than just across a bridge.

Mel Brooks came out to see us during our final week in Cincinnati. As fate and the theatre gods would have it, he saw the show on the night we had the best audience ever. These folks came *in* laughing! They laughed at the *curtain*. They laughed at the *overture*, for Pete's sake!

Afterwards, we all went out for a bite and Mel was like a kid at Christmas as he worked the room. He was thrilled with the show. I'm so fond of Mel. He's like a long-lost eccentric relative.

Now, apparently, word had gotten around that I didn't suck when I went on as Max. One of the higher-ups told me privately that Mel is now claiming he handpicked me from the start. "I knew! I knew! I told them. That Kostroff. I knew it when he walked in!" (That was my Mel impression. Okay, I'm working on it.)

So he says to me: "I heard you were TERRRRRIFIC!!" (Mel talks the way a dog chews on a bone.)

"Oh, well . . . that's great. It was fun, Mel."

"I heard!" he said, wagging a finger at me. "You weren't gonna let that curtain come down!"

"Oh . . . yes . . . well. Thank you." Hell, I didn't know what to say. It was embarrassing, but, geez, how great was it to have Mel Brooks, the man who indirectly taught me how to be funny (I grew up listening to the *2,000 Year Old Man* recordings), mention my name and the word "TERRRRRIFIC" in the same sentence?

Okay, so yadda yadda. Things are great. And since there's not much more to report about Cincinnati, I thought I'd take this opportunity to catch you all up on a few amusing anecdotes from the past few months—stuff I failed to recount the first time around. So here, in random order and with little segue, are some fun bits and pieces:

My sister, her husband, and my two nephews came to Pittsburgh to see the show when we were there. I'm crazy about the nephews. Nick, at nine—the one who reminds me a lot of myself—is becoming quite the little man, and Jason, at five, is fulfilling the main requirement of his age: being hilarious. They showed up in their handsome dress-up clothes, very excited to see Uncle Michael in a show. Beforehand, I gave them a quick backstage tour. Roger, the wig guy, interrupted his pre-show prep to give Nick and Jason their very own Hitler mustaches, which thrilled them to no end, and made the rest of us laugh . . . tensely.

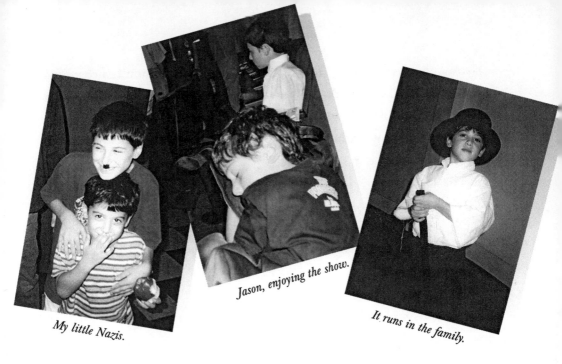

My little Nazis.

Jason, enjoying the show.

It runs in the family.

I explained to them that I played a lot of parts in the show. Their assignment was to see how many times they could find me. (I think the official number of characters is twelve, and I'm often well disguised.)

Afterwards, they were both very excited. Nick had found me every time. And Jason had this to say: "I counted you six times! . . . And then I took a nap!" And that's a great day at the theatre for a five-year-old. You see your uncle, you get a nap in, watch a couple-a' numbers–you're good.

And as we walked to a nearby restaurant for lunch, they competed for who had the better goose step. "I'm a Nazi!" "*No! I'm* a Nazi!!"

At this point my sister had to gently put a stop to things. "Ooooookay, boys. That's enough of that for now. I'll explain later."

Last Sunday, my brother-in-law called to report that the boys have been listening to the CD ever since, and that Jason had just come downstairs dressed as Max Bialystock, the King of Broadway.

When we first meet Franz Liebkind (the insane Nazi playwright of *Springtime for Hitler*), he's on his rooftop, feeding his pet pigeons. The pigeons—puppets operated by unseen ensemble members—are a show unto themselves. One of our swings was watching the show one night, and overheard the following exchange in the lobby during intermission:

> Girlfriend: It was amazing how those pigeons sang and flapped their wings on cue! How do they get those birds to do that?
>
> Boyfriend: *(long, exasperated pause)* Honey . . . they're showbirds. They're *trained* to do that.

Another swing overheard an equally strange remark after "Keep it Gay," the number in which the flaming, notoriously bad stage director, Roger De Bris, introduces his production team, all very gay, including Shirley Markowitz, the butch dyke lighting designer. (Shirley is played by Jessica Sheridan, who, like me, plays several parts in the show.)

> Woman: *(to her husband)* Can you believe they got a real lesbian to play that part?

As you all know, we in the ensemble wear a lot of different costumes. And from time to time, we'll be down in the dressing room getting ready for the next scene and suddenly find ourselves in the wrong outfit. Fellow character man Kevin Ligon and I are the worst. I once saw Kevin dress completely in his colorful second-act Bavarian peasant costume for "Springtime for Hitler" in the middle of Act One, when he's supposed to be a drab accountant. He didn't catch the mistake until he was in full regalia. And of course, as a matter of policy, we never help each other out. It's much more fun to watch someone discover they've put on the wrong costume.

It's easy to get confused. In Act One alone, I'm a highbrow theatre patron, a newspaper man, Leo Bloom's mean boss, a flamingly gay costume designer, and a little old lady!

When the show opens, we're all emerging from the Shubert Theatre, having just seen Max Bialystock's latest flop. The women are in elegant evening gowns, and we men are in tuxes and white gloves. So, a few nights ago, I'm in the dressing room getting ready, chatting away with my fellow ensemble members. I have on my tux, bow tie, patent leather shoes . . . and I look down . . . I'm wearing my little-old-lady purse on my arm and long white little-old-lady gloves. Now there's a look.

Translation, please:

In Cleveland (I shudder at the memory), we had several truly strange comments from audience members. What follows is but one of many bizarre exchanges. I repeat it here in the hopes that someone can tell me what the hell it means:

Audience Member: *(to Lewis J. Stadlen)* Oh, we loved the show!
Lewis: Oh, thank you very much.
Audience Member: You know, we were going to see it on Broadway, but we couldn't get tickets.
Lewis: Well, actually, some people are saying that this is the better production.
Audience Member: Yes . . . we love our town.

Huh?

And finally, this, from cast mate Lee Roy Reams:

"This company is so nice. I mean, I keep waiting to see who the asshole is. I've been in this business a long time and trust me, honey, there's one in every show. But I keep looking and looking . . . I'm starting to think it's me!"

More laughs to come. And maybe we'll even find out who the asshole is.

Stay tuned, friends.
Kostroff

6
HAIL, MARY

Hello, friends.

Greetings once more from out here on the road. Since my last writing, we've moved yet again, this time to Minneapolis, where we're engaged for a four-week run at the Orpheum Theatre.

And here's where we're at:

On Friday, December 6th, the first national tour of *The Producers* gave its 100th performance of the show. The time is flying by. One hundred shows. Seems like only last week we were rehearsing in the sweltering heat of New York City, learning our steps and lines and harmonies. But that was way back in July. Since then, we've packed and unpacked, moved into and out of hotels, flown in airplanes, attended opening night parties, done laundry, seen movies, gotten sick, gotten well again, and entertained thousands and thousands and thousands of theatregoers.

With one exception, we've had a standing ovation every night.

By now, things have fallen into somewhat of a rhythm. Most nights, I plan on getting to the theatre at 7 PM sharp . . . and that puts me there around 7:15. I sign in at the callboard and head for my dressing room, greeting whomever I meet on the way, most of whom I seem to address as "honey" or "doll face," except the boys, of course, who are always "sweetie." Depending on how long we've been in a particular city, I sometimes have to remind myself which hallway to go down.

I change into my warm-up clothes. I finally figured out that I needed them after months of trying to stretch in my jeans. So I went to Target and treated myself to a warm long-sleeved tee shirt and cozy flannel drawstring pants for these colder cities, and added them both to my dressing room supplies so they'd be there waiting for me at each theatre. Putting them on each night has become one of the things I look forward to most, since it fools me into thinking I'm about to go to bed.

I stretch. Sitting on the floor, I can now nearly touch my head to my knee. It's ridiculous. I vocalize a bit while I massage whatever hurts that night. Something always hurts. (Who knew there was an *inner* calf muscle?) I chat with the other members of the male ensemble as they arrive.

We put on our make-up and we talk, joke, and gossip. The stage manager gives the half-hour call over the PA system, and notifies us if any cast members are out that night and, if so, who's replacing them. Sometimes there are other announcements as well: Happy birthday wishes. Posters to sign for charity. "Dollar Friday."* It's the official

---

*"Dollar Friday": A weekly backstage ritual: Members of the company write their names on dollar bills and throw them in a bucket. Then, at intermission, someone (in our company, it's always Pam Bradley, the "Dollar Friday" queen), reaches in and pulls out a bill. Whoever's name is on the bill wins the whole pot.

beginning of the work day. Often, he'll open his announcements with the day and date, which is really helpful, since there's not a man among us who can remember.

At the "five minutes" call, dressed in their robes, the chorus girls go to the stage to rehearse the Glass Pass—a moment in the "I Wanna Be a Producer" number where they have to pass champagne glasses to each other down the line without looking. Apparently, this move is easy to mess up. I think it's ironic that, in a show where we have people flipping, jumping on trampolines, climbing over furniture, doing Russian splits in midair, operating life-sized puppets, riding motorcycles, and dancing on pointe wearing foam rubber military tanks, the Glass Pass has emerged as the one thing that *must* be reviewed each night before curtain.

Those of us in the opening number begin to gather onstage and chat and stretch some more. I always greet our star, Lew Stadlen, and ask how he's doing. The response is usually a grunted "Oy," accompanied by his signature eye roll. I love that guy. The female dancers return, having changed into their evening gowns and looking devastatingly, impossibly pretty. I try to force myself to picture them without make-up. It doesn't help. They're irresistible regardless. And then, from the other side of the curtain, we hear the overture begin. I don't know why, but it always feels so sudden.

The work lights go out. Just to amuse my cast, I often like to dart around the entire length of the empty stage in mock panic screaming, "Oh God! The overture! We'll never be ready!" before getting into position. It was probably amusing the first ten or twenty times. By now, no one even notices. Just part of the pre-show ritual. There goes Kostroff, doing his "we'll never be ready" bit.

And then . . . Oh yes: the show.

After the very brief "Opening Night" number, we all exit, quickly change costumes right in the wings, and reenter immediately as completely different people for the insane "King of Broadway" number. That's the one with the Russian splits. (Not for me, fortunately, though I'm sure the Stroman team could have taught me to do them. As I've said, they have a way of inspiring people. And as a result, I'm already doing things I thought were physically impossible.) So we're all at the top of our abilities, knocking ourselves out: splits, walkovers, coffee grinders, fouettés—you don't even have to know what these things are. You can tell from the sound of them that they're brutal! And the whole time, we're singing. No prerecorded tracks here. It's really us. Singing and dancing our hearts out. The whole thing feels as if we've been blasted out of a cannon.

After the number, we're always panting hard. Good morning! My "going to bed" feeling is suddenly a thing of the past. We all whimper and whine on our way back to the dressing rooms, but the truth is, we love it. It feels really good to work this hard.

I spend most of the rest of my evening changing clothes. At least, that's what it feels like. I get dressed and undressed sixteen times a night, not counting my new warm-up clothes. And by now, it's all routine. The snaps and the Velcro, underdressing* to speed things up, meeting my dresser—different in every city—and Roger, the wig guy, over and over again in various prearranged spots around the backstage area. Funny, how normal this has all become. All those weird outfits—merely status quo. At the same point each night, we all find ourselves standing around in the wings wearing identical blue lace granny dresses with little hats and handbags as we await our entrance for the "Little Old Lady Land" number. Perfectly normal, same old thing, another day at the office, like businessmen waiting for an elevator.

Though the show is taxing, and long, it goes quickly for me now. At the end of the night, we pile out of our costumes as the orchestra plays the "Exit Music." We toss our socks and undershirts into the laundry bins. Before the next show, the dressers will do laundry, steam out shirts and gowns, and reset every single costume in the show. I often think that theirs

---

*underdressing: A wardrobe term for wearing several costumes at once, one on top of another, to facilitate faster changes. The "underdressed" actor can exit the stage, peel off the top layer, and reenter immediately as another character.

is the tougher gig, though I also see them shaking their heads in wonder as they watch us run around all night.

And that's my life these days. So far, I think it agrees with me, this life on the road. I live in hotels, travel constantly, and make a living doing a show that people love every night. Not bad, all in all, in spite of the little aches and the occasional twinges of loneliness.

I find that I take strange comfort lately in national food chains. Somehow, if there's a Rock Bottom Brewery, a Palomino, a P.F. Chang's, even a Denny's, all is well with the world. I may not know where the hell I am, but I know my way around those menus, and the familiarity is grounding. Show people, you may already know, are legendary late-night eaters. Most of us won't *touch* food before a show (in my case, I can't eat for two hours prior to performing), so, after three hours of jumping around like idiots and screaming out songs, we're *famished.* We forget that the world doesn't run by our clock, and so we're appalled when there's an absence of after-hours eateries (and drinkeries) for our post-show needs. To us, it's like some sort of sick, cruel joke. What kind of crazy, backwards city would leave us poor performers stranded with no place to eat dinner at midnight (or, for that matter, breakfast at two in the afternoon)?

Rehearsals continue during the day. Lately, I'm working on my second understudy role, Roger De Bris. They're teaching me more tap steps, and strangely . . . I'm getting them down. Meanwhile, the second covers for the other roles are being taught their parts as well. Fred is going to be a hilarious Max. Since I've already gone on as Max, they don't seem to be too worried about me. And that's rather foolish of them, since I'm still not sure I know what I'm doing.

We've had our first cast change. Our original Carmen Ghia, a truly lovely man, had been having some sort of personal problems. None of us really knows what went on. But he and the producers mutually agreed it was time for him to go home, and I'm convinced that was for the best. It was sad and strange. There was no good-bye. He was just gone one day.

What could we do but wish him well in our hearts and move on? The Carmen Ghia role has been taken over by Michael Paternostro, a wonderful, positive guy who fits right in with our cast. He arrived on a Tuesday and debuted that Friday. He's doing great in the part. The show, as they say, must go on.

Meanwhile, Jennifer, our long-lost chorus girl/Ulla understudy (who, you'll recall, injured her ankle executing The Forbidden Step in rehearsal just before we left New York), has rejoined the company. Good to have her out of her cast and back in ours.

In Minneapolis, there's a statue of Mary Tyler Moore, as Mary Richards, clutching her little bronze purse, throwing her bronze hat into the air, her bronze face smiling hopefully at a bright vision of the future. A group of us stumbled upon her while walking around on our first night in town. Just turned a corner and there she was: the most famous Minneapolisian of all. We all threw our hats into the air. It seemed the right thing to do. Good old Mary. So plucky and positive. She's as apt a symbol as any of how we're feeling these days. We're having fun, enjoying life's adventure. We're turning the world on with our smiles. And if she can brave the cold—even standing out there, day after day and night after night with her hat off—then darn it, Mr. Grant, so can we.

In addition to being officially designated as "America's Most Fun City," as well as the most literate, Minneapolis is home to the Mall of America, which has within its walls not only every imaginable chain restaurant and mall store ever, but also carnival games, two enormous rides that tip you upside down, a Camp Snoopy amusement area for the kids, and yes: a log flume water ride. That's right. *In* the mall. Oh sure. We rode it. Got soaked, forgetting that it was fourteen degrees outside. We had to shop to dry off. Really, what choice did we have? Oh, they're clever.

The downtown area is connected by "skywalks," a network of elevated walkways that take you right through stores, down streets, and over intersections. You could easily spend the whole day downtown and never once go outside, which is what I did more often than not. From my hotel, I could walk to the movie theatre, restaurants, and the two-story Target store, all without even putting on a coat. Now *that's* city planning!

Oh yes. I forgot to mention that Minneapolis is also home to the Target chain. And there's no sales tax on apparel. And I may never leave.

The theatre we played, the Orpheum, looks like it's been there since the heyday of vaudeville. And it probably has. Above the marquee, the name of the theatre is spelled out vertically in huge pink

neon letters, with an ornate purple neon border. It was like a bit of old show biz, saying good night to John the doorman, wrapping my scarf around my neck, and stepping out of the stage door into the falling snow, pink light spilling over the pavement.

It was sharply, thrillingly cold there, and I loved it. Funny, I've never been a cold weather person, and I'm sure I wouldn't like it for very long. (I mean, let's be fair. I only had to walk from my hotel to the theatre, and it was mostly via skywalk.) Even still, I'm reminded of a conversation I had with my nephew Nick, on the occasion of his fifth birthday:

"Okay, so seriously now: You're five. So tell me. Do you think anything changes when you have a birthday? I mean, you were four, and now you're five. What do you think? Do you feel any different?"

And he said:

"Yeah . . . because I used to hate beets, and now I *LOVE* 'em!"

I guess tastes do change as we mature.

Our next stop is St. Louis, and it looks like it's going to be a tough one. Because of a scheduling detail that's too complicated and not interesting enough to explain here, we'll be going thirteen days straight without a day off. So, these next two weeks are going to be a long haul. Lewis has already warned me that I'll probably be going on as Max while we're there. The guy's a trouper, but thirteen days straight is just too much. Especially in that role. Especially after over a hundred performances.

But there's a great big shining light at the end of the St. Louis tunnel! After *two weeks* in St. Louis . . . ah . . . just two short weeks . . . we'll be in San Diego! Not only will it be warm, but I'm told that the hotel is right next to the theatre, and right across from a huge mall. And friends, I'm learning that *that* makes all the difference.

Last night, on our day off, we did a benefit for a wonderful charity called Broadway Cares/Equity Fights AIDS, and I was so very proud of everyone who participated. It was a kick seeing people do different things from what they do in our show every night. Three of our dancers who'd done *Fosse* performed the "Steam Heat" number from *Pajama Game*; Jennifer, one of our brilliant swings, blew the roof off the place with "The Woman in the Moon"; four of us sang my swinging arrangement of "Santa Baby"; and Kevin made us all cry with "Hold On" from *Secret Garden*. It was a full evening of great numbers. Not a clunker in the bunch. And then, the icing on the cake: The entire shebang was emceed by Lee Roy Reams, who . . . well . . . if you don't know him, it's hard to know where to begin. Lee Roy is simply a force of nature. He's been in show business longer than most of us have been alive, knows every show tune, scandalous tale, and filthy joke you can name, and shares *all*. He was a nonstop riot! And we raised some money for an important cause.

I believe Mary would have been proud.

And that's the state of things on the road. Hope all is well with you folks. Please send news of your own adventures. I'm craving stories of the world outside *The Producers*.

Stay warm, wherever you are.

Kostroff

7

A TALE OF TWO CITIES
(OR "A WELL-DESERVED WEST")

January 17th, 2003

Hey, readers,

Life on the road is just full of lessons. And as the months go by, I'm learning more and more about what's really important in life—the really big questions, like: Where's the mall? How close is the theatre? Does the hotel have HBO? Is there laundry in the building? Is there a movie theatre nearby? And most importantly, where the hell are we anyway?

These are the very considerations that made St. Louis a bit of a schlep. The hotel was far from the theatre, so we had to be bused back and forth each day. And there wasn't much to do in either neighborhood. If we wanted to go somewhere, we had to take a cab. Sometimes we did. But most of the time, we hung out at the hotel.

The much-anticipated Welden Hotel in St. Louis is only a year old. We'd heard that the cast of *Mamma Mia!* loved it so much that after checking in, they came back to the lobby to hug their company managers, who'd found the place. And indeed, it looked great. The lobby was trendily designed, with modern, oversized couches and funky lamps, a plum-colored pool table, a sleek restaurant with a shiny metal bar, and nonstop music. The rooms were like luxury apartments, with separate bedrooms, full kitchens, huge TVs, Japanese flower and bamboo arrangements, and Jacuzzi tubs!

Heaven? Not so fast. The Welden was, in a word, a bimbo—beautiful but dumb. Run by the party animal son who shares ownership with his elderly father, it was a mess just below the surface. The young, way-too-attractive staff seemed overwhelmed by the simplest questions. Dining in the restaurant the first day, I asked the waiter what the soup of the day was.

Waiter: *(pause)* . . . Soup?
Michael: Yes, the soup. The soup of the day? What kind is it?
Waiter: Oh, you mean the soup of the day?
Michael: Yes, that's it. Today's soup.
Waiter: *(wrinkling his model-perfect face in deep concentration)* Ummm . . .
    I don't really know.

This was followed by a lonnnng silence.

Waiter: Like . . . did you want me to ask the chef? Or . . .
Michael: Yes. That might be a good thing to know. You know, in case
    anyone else asks you.
Waiter: Oh, yeah.

I suppose I shouldn't be too harsh. He didn't look like he ate often, and so perhaps he wasn't well acquainted with food items, per se. And with three whole tables to wait on, it was hard to handle "special requests" like information about the menu or cream for the coffee.

And those Jacuzzi tubs? Never enough hot water to fill them. It was such a tease. You'd get yourself all ready for a good, steamy soak. You'd crank the faucet, full throttle, expecting a scalding Niagara.

Instead, you'd get a half-hearted stream of briefly hot water—about enough to fill six or seven inches of the sprawling tub. After that, the water quickly turned cold—always . . . *always* . . . just short of the jets. So you had a choice: Take a cool-to-tepid Jacuzzi, or do your best to paste yourself against the porcelain for the shallowest hot bath you've ever known.

The beautiful kitchens were missing basic amenities: things like toasters and can openers and plates. Lavish amounts of cupboard space. Nothing in them.

At the front desk, the answer to every question was, "I don't know," with no attempt to find out.

"What time does the mail go out?"

"I don't know *(sexy pout)*."

"Is there a Kinko's near by?"

"I don't know *(sexy pout)*."

"Is there someone we can ask?"

"I don't know *(sexy pout)*. But I like your shirt. Is it Hilfiger?"

"It's Target, but thank you."

Printed materials were filled with typos. (You know how I get about *that*.) In the elevator, an ad for the hotel's New Year's Eve celebration listed "Complimentory Champaign" among its many misspelled features.

It was even hard to get a telephone line out. If three hotel guests were talking on their room phones, you got a busy signal.

There was, hidden among the airhead staff, one very bright, very competent, very helpful assistant hotel manager. The day before we left, she was fired.

There was just something weird about this place. Most of the time, it was like a ghost town. Just us and the staff, who all lived there. And then some nights, we'd come dragging in after the show to find the place *hopping*! Casino game tables set up, themed décor, big groups of people we'd never seen before draped all over the bar area. Dancing. Laughter. And then, the next day . . . whoooosh. No one. Bizarre.

Then, one night, at four in the morning, one of our dancers woke to find three guys drunkenly stumbling into her room, carrying an ice bucket.

Melanie: Uh . . . hello?

Dumb Drunk Guy: Oh . . . hey . . . The owner said we could come up here and party.

Melanie: You have the wrong room!

DDG: Isn't this 410?

Melanie: YOU HAVE THE WRONG ROOM!

DDG: Oh . . . okay.

And they left. Now, what makes this even stranger is this: Melanie had her door locked. There was only one key that could have gotten past that lock. The master key. And who had a copy? You guessed it. The party animal owner. And while we're playing Columbo, why weren't the dumb drunk guys surprised and apologetic when they saw a girl in the room? Were they *expecting* to find a girl in the room? What the hell kind of place *is* this? (And why the hell wasn't there a girl in *my* room . . . oh . . . uh . . . I mean . . . Anyway . . .)

The next day, as all hell broke loose over the incident (they ended up comping Melanie's stay and she moved elsewhere), it came out that this idiot had given the key to his friends and mistakenly told them the room was empty. To this day, no one has apologized. The owner did, however, offer to buy us all drinks after the show one night. I don't think any of us went.

So that was the story of the Welden (which, of course, isn't its real name).

The run in St. Louis did have its good points:

We had snow, which was gorgeous, and Christmas, which was . . . well, you know . . . kind of fun, kind of lonely. Most people had family visiting. I'm estranged from mine. But it was fine. I liked that we had a matinee on Christmas Eve and an evening performance Christmas Day. Not being much for holidays, I've always loved working on those days, entertaining the people who are celebrating. On Christmas Eve itself, we had a big dinner at the hotel. It was a very warm feeling, sharing a night off and relaxing together as a company.

I chose not to do the Secret Santa thing, because I knew watching from the sidelines would be even more fun! I loved seeing people sneak around leaving gifts, clues, poems, and so on. Everyone was very creative. Jen Lee is our dance captain. Her Secret Santa started out by leaving her wonderful gifts . . . and then he turned evil. One night, he left her a fake red nose, and a note instructing her to wear it while singing and dancing "Rudolph the Red Nosed Reindeer" at five minutes to curtain, or risk being cut off from receiving any more gifts. On another night, she had to talk all in rhymes. It was hilarious. Poor Jen. She loved every minute of it. Her secretly sadistic Santa turned out to be none other than the mischievous, gregarious Michael Goddard. And if you knew him, you wouldn't be the least bit surprised.

The theatre we played, the Fox, was beyond beautiful, and enormous: It seats close to 5,000 people. I don't know what you'd call the style. Byzantine-Egyptian-Moroccan-Rococco-Flambé-Supreme or something. You cannot imagine the outrageously ornate detail of this unique, old, renovated movie palace. There were carvings of gods, Chinese fans, sprawling leaves, musical instruments, mythical animals . . . more than your eyes could take in, all in shining gold. There were gold-bordered ceiling insets, lit in vivid colors from within, and a deep magenta curtain of heavy velvet. And, high above the proscenium, a huge bronze elephant presided, its trunk protruding out over the audience.

Way at the back of the house and one floor up was the Club Level, where VIPs could arrive early to dine, then watch the show—all from the privacy of their own booths, each equipped with a call light for the cocktail waiter, in case they needed to freshen up their drinks during the show. Posh, posh, posh. They were miles away from the stage, but then, these folks probably have opera glasses.

It was a tricky house to play, particularly for comedy. The room was so vast that there was an actual time delay between the punch lines and the laughs. So it was tough to gauge. Cast mate Nancy Johnston says it was like listening to people at a party across the lake. You could tell they were having a good time, but you weren't quite sure what they were laughing at.

It was the sort of place that you could easily believe was filled with old ghosts. Kind of *Phantom of the Opera* without the tragedy. The male ensemble dressing room was one level down, directly below the stage. For each entrance, we climbed an old metal

The Fox Theatre, St. Louis. Photo: Sam Fentress.

stairway right up through the stage floor in the wings. It was very cool, like being on a ship or something. And there were what seemed like *hundreds* of doors and passageways. Where did they all lead?

And all throughout the backstage areas of the building, along the halls on every floor, painted right onto the walls, mural-style, were recreations of posters for every show that's ever played the Fox. Some of them are quite involved. The ambitious artist of the *Dreamgirls* mural attached wigs, sequins, and feather boas to her life-sized painting of the three leads. Each mural is signed by its show's cast. As I roamed the halls, exploring, I even found signatures of friends and past associates on those walls. Small world.

Since the logo for *The Producers* is a door, two of our artistically talented company members converted a real door into our mural. They added a fake mail slot and painted the handle to look like brass, and then we all signed. If you ever play the Fox in St. Louis, you'll find us there . . . part of its history.

Even with these few highlights, the company was dragging. We were cold, tired, and lacking for diversion, stranded as we were within the confines of the luxuriously frustrating Welden. And there had been various strains of the flu, allergies, injuries, and a general sense of burnout. We were doing our best to keep ourselves together and keep the show looking good, but we desperately needed relief.

And then came San Diego.

(Music up. Angels singing. Blinding sunset. An ocean breeze.)

After thirteen days in St. Louis without a break, we packed up our luggage and dragged ourselves to the airport, tired, cold, and wiped out, boarded a plane, and landed, just a few hours later, in perfect San Diego.

We stumbled, squinting at the sunlight, into the seventy-two-degree hug that hung in the air, like frozen Polish refugees who'd won a luxury vacation in the Caribbean. Everyone looked almost confused by the gorgeousness. Lost in wonder at our tremendous fortune, yet not quite trusting that it was real, we cautiously shed our coats and sweaters and fell, gratefully, into our beds at the Westgate Hotel.

Now, the Westgate is everything the Welden wasn't. The owner is Austrian, so it's very old-world. Everything is decorated in the Baroque style. The staff is made up largely of young people who have come over from Austria for an eighteen-month training program, so the service is state-of-the-art. (*They* can tell you the soup of the day in several *languages*!) They're lovely. There's a daily afternoon tea, with a *harpist*, if you please. And wait, it gets better. The theatre is around the corner! The mall, complete with movie theatre, is across the street! There are restaurants everywhere! Pinch me! I must be dreaming! I'm in tour heaven!

Since the distance to San Diego was considerably further than our other jumps, it took several days for the trucks to arrive with our sets and costumes. So we were forced to take three days off instead of one. Oh, how we suffer. (Rest assured, they made up the performances later in the week with a few extra matinees, but none of us minded.) The company splintered off to see friends, soak in mud baths, and generally recharge. Daniel, our Nazi Tenor, and Don, our conductor, had discovered a common love of horses, so off they went to go riding at Don's ranch in nearby Temecula.

As for me, I was yearning for life outside the show. And so off *I* went, on our first night in town, to see my great pal Ame, her two terrific kids, Zach and Gillian, their cute new dog, Casper, and Ame's mom, Joy, who was visiting with her friend, Ross. When I arrived, the grown-ups were all painting Gillian's room. (I helped by sitting on the floor and watching.) It was so soothing and homey—miles away from the theatre, catching up with friends. Ame made dinner, and we all sat and laughed and drank wine and told of our adventures. A home-cooked meal! In an actual house, with rooms and everything! And kids and a dog and a mom! Man—after months on the road, I needed that.

But my main activity during the extra days off was nursing the impressive shin splints I'd developed in St. Louis. I'd been dancing in spite of them (of course) and ooooh, did they hurt. Massage had become a necessity, along with ice, Advil, and Epsom salt baths in the few inches of hot water I could squeeze out of the Welden Hotel's tub. Now, in San Diego, my shins enjoyed a much-needed break. I walked a little, but no big adventures. And at this writing, they're much better. Truthfully, there's a part of me that loves my shin splints. It's kind of that tough, show-must-go-on, "theatre-ain't-pretty-now-get-out-there-and-sell-it" thing. But my extra tap-dancing rehearsals for the Roger De Bris role drastically diminished their charm. Ouuuuuch. Upon touching my shins for the first time, the first of several massage therapists gasped with alarm, "My goodness! It's as if your legs are made of wood!"

"I know," I responded, "but I hope one day to be a real boy."

The audiences in San Diego turned out to be, by far, the best we've had. While audiences in other cities occasionally had to be spoon-fed, the San Diegans were laughing halfway through the punch lines! They even got the most "inside" jokes. It was a party.

Friends drove down from LA to see me, which was like a belated Christmas present. It was so good visiting with them all. I was lunching one day with friends Kathy and Florene. They'd just seen the matinee and we were talking about the show over salads when my cell phone rang. I thought I'd better answer, in case it was something urgent.

Me: Uh-huh . . . Uh-huh . . . Okay . . . No problem . . . Uh-huh . . . Okay. Bye. *(to Kathy and Florene)* Well, Lew's out sick. I'm playing the lead tonight.
Kathy: Oh, my! Wow!
Florene: Just like that?!?!!
Me: Yep.

Well, that was even better than the show! They flipped! I loved having witnesses when the "Batphone" rang—always an exciting call. Having been on a few times before, I was fairly calm, but I was glad I'd ordered only salad!

I loved getting to play Max Bialystock in San Diego. The audience was so warm. And they seemed to really get into rooting for the understudy. They laughed at my very first punch line, and didn't stop laughing for the next three hours. This was definitely a theatre town.

For some reason, San Diego was also the city where we had a strange run of technical difficulties. Maybe all that powerful laughter shook the building too much. One night, as we were heading into the home stretch, the set crashed. Now, for those of you who've never seen a Susan Stroman show, transitions are one of her specialties. She's a genius at getting from one scene to the next. At the point in question, the Shubert Theatre set is, in theory, sliding in behind the prison backdrop while the "Prisoners of Love" number is happening onstage. Normally, the backdrop rises and we "prisoners" dance off through the Shubert's stage door. But on this particular night, the Shubert ran aground. That is to say, another set piece somehow pushed it off its track, leaving it wedged in the wings. So the first dancing prisoner, finding only space where the set usually is, invented new, impromptu choreography, strutting confidently off in a jazz run. The rest of us immediately followed, as if we'd done it every night, and we finished the show Shubertless.

Since then we've had several smaller glitches. One night, someone forgot to set FDR's wheelchair, so he hobbled, on foot, across the stage. (Good thing I was offstage for that one. I don't think I could have kept a straight face.) Another night, our motorcycle (which travels on a small track) came on, but wouldn't go off. There it stayed, stuck, in full view. The rider—who had to get to his next quick costume change—had no choice but to abandon his vehicle and walk the rest of the way, leaving it to the stagehands to sneak out and push the darn thing, finally, into the wings.

But probably the funniest was The Night the Curtain Went Up Early. We were all in the midst of our pre-show ritual: stretching and chatting onstage, as we do every night, when we suddenly became aware that we were . . . not alone. Someone had pushed the wrong button, and the curtain was going up. The audience, after a stunned moment, decided it was part of the show and began to chuckle and applaud. My good buddy Pam Bradley, who was doubled over, legs in a wide stance, touching her toes, with her rear end to our public, was among the last to notice. Most of the cast, being the seasoned, dignified professionals we are, screamed and ran into the wings. We were only in view for a few seconds, but it was a good ten minutes into the show before we regained our dignity. Since then, I've noticed, we've all had one eye on the curtain beginning around 7:55. And Pam has begun to stretch facing the opposite direction.

On New Year's Eve, I broke a long-standing tradition. I was, for the first time in well over a decade, out among people. Now, normally, I hide. People get crazy and out of control on New Year's Eve. And besides that, I'm perpetually single, and with no one to kiss at midnight, what's the point? So, to avoid the crowds and potential despair, I have a tradition of my own: I hole up in my apartment and sort my receipts. Now that may sound bleak, but I like it! It's my own nostalgic ritual. I go back through the year, recalling meals with friends, shows, trips, and other events. Puts a cap on things.

But this year, as an experiment, I socialized. I spent the evening with a handful of cast mates, all of us wedged into the tiny, butterscotch-colored bar at the Westgate. They'd convinced me to abandon my curmudgeonly ways regarding the holiday. Well, why not? Change is good . . . ?

A full fourth of the little room was taken up by a grand piano, where a woman was singing, accompanied by–I swear it–a gypsy violinist. I don't make this stuff up, people. It was wonderfully odd, and we had to chuckle at some of their song choices. (I don't know . . . somehow, as a single person in my forties, "Send in the Clowns" isn't really what I want to hear on New Year's Eve. You might as well sing "Is That All There Is?" or "You're Nobody Till Somebody Loves You.") Everyone's spouses and mates were there, and they all kissed romantically at midnight. And I watched them, wistfully, while balloons fell on my head. Wheee. Big fun. So glad I left my room for this.

Eh . . . whatcha gonna do? It was sweet to see them all happy and celebrating.

Next year, I go back into hiding.

Anyway, that's the update from the road. There'll be more adventures to come as we wend our way north towards San Francisco, then back down to Los Angeles. For the moment, we find ourselves in Tempe, Arizona . . .

. . . but that's another story.

Kostroff

8
THROUGH THE DESERT

February 4th, 2003

Dear friends,

I always enjoy moving day. Every few weeks, just as things are becoming routine, we fold up our tents and take our little traveling circus back out on the road. There's an excitement about it: new city, new hotel, new theatre, new dressing rooms, and a new audience to entertain.

Late at night on the Friday before we leave, we all push our trunks outside our hotel room doors and, sometime early the next morning, while we sleep, big strong guys whisk them away and throw them onto a truck bound for the next city. It's just like leaving a tooth under your pillow for the Tooth Fairy and waking up to find . . . well . . . change.

A few days later, the trunks mysteriously appear outside our doors at the next hotel, miles away.

And somewhere in between those two events, we're whisked away as well.

On moving day we usually gather at around 10 AM—an hour that exists purely in fiction for show people—dragging our suitcases and computers and even pets (some company members are touring with animal pals). It's our day off, so we tend to keep quietly to ourselves and rest our brains and voices, particularly because we're not quite awake. While I'm less than crazy about flying, the change of scenery upon arrival is a great payoff. I like moving into the new hotel room—my home for the next several weeks—putting things away, stowing my suitcases, and taking a walk around the new neighborhood.

In fact, it's become one of my traditions to stroll by the theatre on that first night in town—the night before we open—and snoop around. I watch as the trucks are unloaded and pieces of the show are installed. I like seeing the unlit marquee, and looking through the doors into the darkened lobby, knowing that the very next night the place will be filled with light and buzzing with anticipation as our opening night crowd and local reviewers get their tickets, file in, and take their seats.

For the move from San Diego to Tempe, Arizona, I did something different. I decided to join Jessica Sheridan—character actress extraordinaire—in renting a car and driving while most of the company flew. It turned out to be a great choice. The six-hour drive was restful and beautiful, and, while the main subject of conversation was work (it usually is among the cast), Jessica and I also found the opportunity to talk about life outside of the show.

So we're driving through the desert, chatting, bonding, enjoying the warm air and the views of red rocks and cacti . . .

. . . when suddenly, the phone calls started coming in . . .

The majority of our cast, already in Tempe, had found the Empire Suites hotel completely unlivable. "I don't know what kind of emperor would stay here," laughed Kevin over my cell phone. "We're all sitting here outside trying to figure out what to do." According to the colorful reports that followed from various cast mates, the place was horribly dark and dirty, with a surly staff and an unidentifiable stench. The small rooms had one tiny window each. It sounded like a medieval prison! One by one, company members had returned to the front desk and checked back out. (You know it had to be bad for the reaction to be so unanimous.) There they were, with all their stuff, ready to settle in and get something to eat. Now they had to find another place to stay for the next three weeks. Fortunately, it sounded like they all had a sense of humor about it.

Jessica and I drove along, chuckling with selfish glee that we'd dodged this housing disaster, all of which would be completely worked out by the time we got there. What good fortune to be breezing through the desert, miles away from the insanity, enjoying the view.

A bit further down the road, we got an update: The company had gotten organized. They were on a mission. Everyone had squeezed into the few cars among them, piled the luggage high, put dogs on laps, and struck out in different directions, keeping in touch by cell phone to report their findings. It was a mad scramble to find someplace comfortable that would offer a decent rate.

Lah-dee-dah. Jessica and I stopped for a leisurely bite, then continued on. Our phones were quiet for a while. Then came the latest: Everyone had decided to settle at a place called the Studio 6. "It's smaller than any place we've ever stayed," Melissa told me. "But it's clean and bright and the staff is nice, and it's thirty-five bucks a night, so there you go." I called ahead and reserved rooms for Jessica and myself.

Shortly after sunset, we pulled up to the Studio 6 in Tempe. Melissa's description had been absolutely accurate. The staff was nicer and far more accommodating than one would expect to find at an economy motel. But it was an economy motel. Tiny room, tiny efficiency kitchen. White walls. No art. No frills. No kidding. One plastic plant. We dropped our stuff and went shopping for groceries.

Now, I think it's only right for a traveling theatrical such as myself to develop some eccentricities. One's public, not to mention the tabloids, comes to expect such things. And it makes even the most boring among us at least somewhat intriguing. In my case, I find I'm developing–or maybe just dis-covering–a respectable number of oddities, one of which is that I hate . . . no . . . *loathe* . . . fluorescent light. And when I say loathe, I want you to picture Herbert Lom's expression every time the name "Clouseau" was mentioned in the *Pink Panther* movies. Remember how one eye would twitch and the opposite cheek would quiver, like he'd gotten bad news while eating a grapefruit? That's the look. The intensity of my feelings on the subject approaches the wild-eyed fervor of a conspiracy theorist. It's my belief that fluorescent light robs the body of vitamins, saps the energy, causes depression, restlessness, gout, dry heaves, and rickets, and emits an invisible beacon that shows the aliens where to land so they can steal your intestines.

I could be wrong about that last part.

Now, in recent years I've noticed a disturbing trend in even the best hotels of replacing nice, normal, evil-free light bulbs with the cheaper, inherently sinister kind. So when I move into a new room, one of the first things I do is to peer suspiciously over the lampshades, and if the horrible little things are present, I exclaim "Aha!" as if the hotel management was trying to put one over on me. I've learned how to remove them. Oh, they're clever, but not clever enough for me. I'm sure I'm risking some sort of fine, but I don't care. Once the poisonous illuminators have been yanked from their little sockets, I march, with no small degree of righteous indignation, to the nearest store, where I purchase several normal light bulbs, and damn the cost. Hell, I've even gone as high as three bucks. But what's money, when weighed against the importance of my intestines? Trick me, will you? Well they've got another thing coming.

I need hardly tell you that the room at the Studio 6 was fluorescent everywhere you looked. I set that right but quick. And while I was at it, I bought my usual food staples. And so, we were all settled in for our run in Tempe . . . or so it seemed.

But, over the next few days, there was restlessness at the Studio 6. Several of us, having hastily taken refuge there, were beginning to question whether such a small space would be comfortable for three weeks. So, after some characteristic waffling (does that qualify as an eccentricity?), I packed up my food and my clothes and my light bulbs and transferred to the nearby Residence Inn, where I got a room with a fireplace and lots of windows, and where I was very comfortable . . . once I'd replaced the fluorescents.

I felt so bad for Diane, the manager of the Studio 6. One day, she has a sudden, unexpected flood of business. Two days later, half of them check out. This is how show people get a bad reputation.

As we got into our Tempe run, I sensed that, while the weather was lovely and warm and everyone was, ultimately, happy with their housing, things had gotten a bit dry with the show. Not bad, just kind of . . . eh. And it seemed to be a time when for a lot of us, being in the first national tour of the biggest Broadway hit in years was just a job. A good job. An enjoyable job. But still, a job. And that was fine. These things go in cycles, and right now we were in a dry phase . . . dry and flat. We were going through the desert, both literally and metaphorically.

The audiences were drier too, compared with those wonderful crowds in San Diego. Now, mind you, we've never had an audience yet that didn't love the show. But there are varying degrees. And these folks weren't quite as wild in their response as in other cities. And that was fine too. This I've learned: It can't be utter bliss all the time.

The theatre, the Gammage Auditorium, is on the campus of Arizona State University. One of our swings, Michael Goddard (who, you may recall, was the Sadistic Secret Santa of St. Louis) went to school there, so he was a sudden celebrity: interviewed all over town for newspapers and radio, greeted nearly every night at the stage door by some relative or friend, and he even had a musical theatre student from ASU—his protégé—who followed him everywhere, soaking up his professional guidance. Now Michael is . . . well, you'd have to meet him. He's one of those fabulous, gregarious, larger-than-life personalities. He's like the company cruise director, always coming up with activities and outings. He's Party Central. Whenever we have a holiday gathering or something, Michael's the one who proposes the toast. That's just him. So we hardly batted an eye when he swept into the dressing room one night and announced, "Boys, we've been invited to a party at the mayor's house. Friday after the show. It's fabulous. You all have to come."

That's right. The mayor of Tempe. Now, whatever mayoral image just popped into your mind, erase it. This mayor was young, handsome . . . and openly gay. No suit, no tie, no bifocals. He's been mayor for something like eight years, and I got the feeling that gatherings at his house weren't unusual. The mayor has a lot of friends.

The party at which we found ourselves was like bring-a-friend night at a gay disco. Our cast members made up only a small part of the crowd that squeezed into the mayor's stylish little house. People oozed through the main room and out around the pool as house music thump-thump-thumped above our heads. We all got snacks and drinks and started casing the joint, pausing for several minutes in the master bathroom to ponder the curvy, tiled shower that was big enough for three people.

It was a really nice group of locals. No one was standoffish. Surprisingly few had seen the show, and not all of them knew it was playing in town. ("It's a *musical*. Are you sure you people are gay?" I thought.) All the same, they seemed happy to meet us, and the whole evening made for a great diversion.

As the weeks went on, the audiences got better. That seems to happen consistently. We think it's because the earlier audiences in each city are sub-scribers, who come to the show because it's part of the theatre's season. Later in the runs, audiences are made up of people who specifically bought tickets to see *The Producers*, so they're a bit livelier.

One night, in the usual pre-show hustle and bustle of the men's dressing room, fellow ensemble member Robin Lewis and I were talk-ing about a director we both know, Michael Barnard. "Where is he these days?" Robin asked.

"I think he's some-where in Arizona." I said.

There was a chuckle from my left. "Kostroff," said Kevin, "We're *in* Arizona."

ASU's Gammage Auditorium, designed by Frank Lloyd Wright.

"Oh! We are? Oh yes! That's right! I'll have to call him."

Michael Barnard is one of the best directors I've ever worked with. He directed that production of *Forum* I told you about in my Cleveland report (the one where I was unexpectedly moved into the lead). That experience helped prepare me for what I'm doing now; in going on as Max, I've often leaned on the things I learned from Michael, and the confidence he inspired. He'd pushed me. Hard. And I appreciated it now more than ever. "If you're doing this right," he once told me, "you'll be eating steak at midnight, and *still* be losing weight."

These days, Michael is running a theatre in Phoenix. It was dragging when he took over. But he turned it around, and now it's exceeding its goals. Not surprising. He's a very talented guy. As I've gone along, I've realized how rare great directors like Michael are. So I was really happy to track him down, go out for dinner, and tell him how influential he'd been. He came to see the show, and we laughed and reminisced and caught up. And I felt like he was proud of me, which meant a lot.

So, between visits with friends, the disco party at the mayor's pad, and various other adventures, the cast's trip through the desert was dotted with enough oases to sustain us. And after all, it was great to be in such a nice, warm place in the middle of January. In fact, I suppose, we could have been tempted to stay. But by now, the Trunk Fairy had once again visited our rooms as we slept, and it was time once again to move on, this time to Seattle, land of coffee and rain, which promised to be just the magic combination we needed: an energizing caffeine jolt to wake us up, and moisture from the heavens to end our dry spell.

Keep in touch, friends.
Kostroff

9
COOKIE JARS AND NUTTY RUSSIANS

February 21st, 2003

We're in the holding pattern. That's the name of the step. Stroman and her team like to name everything to make it easier to remember, and it works. It gives us a kind of shorthand for the choreography. "Howdy Neighbor," for example, is a tap step where both hands go up in the air as you face your partner. "Here's to You" is when the showgirls toast with their champagne glasses. We've also got "Chinese Ladies," "Nutty Russians," and "Yiddish Muppets." And my favorite name, "Dance for the Deaf," is shorthand for the series of gestures that accompany the lyric, "*adios/au revoir/wiedersehn/ ta-ta-ta/goodbye/get lost/get out!*" in our final number, "Goodbye."

The "Holding Pattern," then, is a step in "King of Broadway" where we all rock back and forth while Max speaks. From my spot in the "Holding Pattern," peripherally, I can see several of my cast mates, some of the crew in the wings, the conductor, the lights, and a bit of that vast, dark ocean of people out there, nearly invisible at that point, except for the reflection of eyeglasses and a few front row faces. And for some reason, lately, it's at this brief moment in the show that I've been thinking how swell it is to be singing and dancing onstage in a big national tour. And I get a twinge of pride, as I "Holding Pattern" for all I'm worth, thinking of the thousands of people who've been entertained by our little "skit," as we like to call it. Lately, that's just the point where it hits me. Hot damn! Look where I am: I'm touring in *The Producers*!

It's in that same moment that I'm often struck by "the *Groundhog Day* factor" (our newly coined term, named for the Bill Murray movie in which he repeats the same day over and over again, unable to get out of it). Here I am, I think to myself, doing the "Holding Pattern" . . . AGAIN! We've done the "Holding Pattern" in St. Louis, in Minneapolis, in Tempe, in Cleveland. We've done it twice a day on the weekends—every weekend, for the past six months. We've done it with injuries, with attitudes, in silly moods, with rediscovered excitement, with new orchestras who were playing a bit too fast, on opening nights and closing nights and the nights in between. But we've done it every show. Over and over and over again. And then over and over and over again some more. And for the audience, we have to make each time look like the first time . . . again, and again, and again. *Groundhog Day*. Sometimes, we get to feeling utterly punch-drunk from the repetition. There's a bit of madness about it: Didn't we just do this?

We're in Seattle now. We'll play here for two weeks, then Portland for two, then San Francisco for eight, and then we'll be in LA, where I'll be back in my own apartment, which will be great. I think we're all looking forward to unpacking and settling in for a few months.

It's in San Francisco that we'll begin rehearsals with Jason Alexander and Martin Short, who will step into the roles of Max and Leo for our LA run. And we've recently learned that Gary Beach, who originated the Roger De Bris role on Broadway (a performance for which he won a Tony Award) will also be joining us, as will a new Carmen Ghia, Josh Prince. (Our beloved Michael Paternostro, who plays the role currently, has opted out of LA, and our wonderful Lee Roy Reams, who currently plays De Bris, has been asked to help launch the second national tour.)

And so, our little family will soon be breaking up. And yet, we look forward to working with the new guys. Happy news and sad news, all at once.

Meanwhile, we're in a holding pattern.

Seattle's a great town. And we could have easily stayed here longer, both in terms of the company's "druthers" and in terms of how well the show is selling. But prior to opening there was, I feel, a hair of skepticism about our great big Broadway smash on the part of this hip, grungy, brooding, bohemian Mecca.

The day before the show opened, I stopped by a coffee house for a bite to eat and picked up a copy of *Seattle Weekly*, the local, free, hip, "alternative" newspaper. Paging through the theatre section to get a sense of the city's artistic "vibe," I scanned a few of the reviews of local stage productions. While *A Chorus Line* was mercilessly panned, as were several light comedies, the tragic, cutting-edge new drama about the headless circus performer dealing with his sexuality issues (yes, really) garnered an absolute "this is what theatre is all about" rave. Oh, we were in big trouble. And then, to my surprise, my eye fell on a blurb about *The Producers*. Strange, I thought. We hadn't opened yet. Thought you'd enjoy reading it:

Call it the Broadway equivalent of Hollywood's *Titanic*—it's The Blockbuster That Will Have You Whether or Not You Will Have It. Mel Brooks' 2001 musical . . . won more Tony Awards than any other show in history (is this thing really better than, say, *West Side Story*? Than *Gypsy*?), and has typically sober old critics gushing like wet toddlers and audiences primed to be wowed, dammit, or else perceived as killjoys. Seattle theatregoers have already got the Paramount going *ka-ching*. The first day of ticket sales—$359,564—was the theatre's highest ever for a Broadway show. Who knew that the irreverent tale of two schmucks trying to scam investors with a god-awful musical about the Führer would, in fact, pay off so handsomely? And, OK. Maybe the damn thing is all that. Whatever, the juggernaut that is the national tour hits town today, and you can safely expect anyone with expendable income and a *New York Times* subscription to be singing "Springtime for Hitler" for the next week and a half.

—*Steve Wiecking*, Seattle Weekly, *2/5/2003*

Ooh . . . it sounded like they were poised to hate us. I had this image of our cast, standing on the stage, getting pelted by umbrellas, coffee beans, knit caps, and grunge CDs. But when the show actually opened, it opened to very appreciative crowds—not a curmudgeon in the bunch—who would have happily kept us running for months, rather than weeks. Those who weren't too hip to be seen there seemed to have been waiting with great excitement for the show's arrival in town. And the reviews? Well, they tried not to like it, but what can you do? Whether or not you think this show is brilliant, there's no denying it's invincible.

My favorite review was the one that confused me with Michael Paternostro, calling me "svelte and sassy." It was the first—and last—time I've ever been described using those words.

Meanwhile, we've seen none of the legendary incessant rain you're always hearing about. (Seattleites, I've found, are particularly irritable on this point. "It *doesn't* rain all the *time!*" they'll tell you defensively. "That's just a *rumor.*") The theatre is beautiful. The audiences are terrific. The hotel is great. And Seattle, as I said, is a great town. I made a point to stroll down to the famous Pike Place Fish Market and yes, they really do throw the fish. One guy takes the order and calls to the guy in the back, who throws these huge raw fish to the guy at the counter. And that was really all the entertainment I needed. Just like *The Producers*, it's quite a show.

We had only one day off here, which I spent with Lee Roy and (assistant stage manager) Liza, looking at antiques . . . . .Antiques . . . . Okay, I'm not really sure how that happened. I don't even like antiques.

One night, in the middle of the show, as we hastily passed each other in a backstage hallway, Lee Roy invited me to join a "group of us" for some sort of expedition. Some town called Snohomish . . . or something. "Sure!" I said as I dashed down the hall to my next costume change, not knowing exactly where we were headed. Now, several cast mates had gone to a place called Snoqualmie Falls and returned with stories of sights too beautiful to miss, and, well, I guess I didn't listen to the name all that carefully. I mean, all those Indian names sound alike, right? I figured that if it wasn't the actual Falls, it must be close, since the name was at least similar. You know, like New York and New Delhi, Van Nuys and Vancouver, Akron and Akbar . . . same difference, right? Oh, I'm very smart.

But after all, Lee Roy Reams is Broadway royalty. He's been in show business for ages (looks *fantastic*, by the way), and can tell you wild stories about the most famous people in theatre, because he's worked with them all. ("Lupe Velez! Oh come on, you've heard of Lupe Velez! Died with her head in the toilet. You *know* this!") You don't turn down an opportunity to hang out with the legendary Mr. Reams.

So I found myself, way too early the following Monday, motoring along in the passenger seat of Lee Roy's rental car. "Now, *where* are we going again?" I muttered in my sleep, rubbing my eyes and yawning, my undercaffeinated brain trying to piece together why I'd tagged along.

"Snohomish! Oh I hear it's fabulous! A whole street of antique stores!" Now, unlike me, Lee Roy *loves* antiques. *Loves* 'em. He has a houseful back home. Piles and piles of the stuff. Especially anything having to do with Dachshunds. He collects them. With a passion. ("Why Dachshunds?" I asked, to which he responded, "Well, because I have two of them at home, you see." Silly me.)

I looked to Liza in the back seat for any help at all in solving the mystery of why we were there. She just shrugged.

Well, what the hell? Too late to turn back now. And, in truth, the day was far from torturous. We wandered, chatted, stopped to eat, and so on. And Lee Roy and Liza are both great company. But I found that, on our day of rest, trying to mentally process case after case after case of tchotchkes–thousands upon thousands of . . . *things*–wore me out!

There were rusty old wind-up toys, tea cozies, suitcases, pillbox hats, shoe trees, place mats, posters, rings, tumblers, paperweights, golf clubs, bolts of fabric, milk bottles, canes, LPs, frames, cookie jars, flatware, high chairs, bow ties, paintings, mirrors, books, thimbles, lamps . . . Store after store, floor after floor, case after case. My brain spun at the sight of it all as I stood before each thing, gawking. What am I supposed to be doing here, exactly? Deciding whether or not I *need* the froggy salt and pepper shakers? Or just looking at them, like paintings in a museum? My God. All this stuff. Americans love our stuff, don't we? And these towering emporiums were like temples, paying homage to great mountains of old stuff. Old stuff that people used to own. Cases and cases of it. And shelves and racks and piles and rooms.

Anyway, I shlumped along. And some of the stuff was really cool. And sometimes, I'd just step outside for some Snohomish air while Lee Roy regaled a shopkeeper with some ribald tale or other about a Broadway star of the Golden Age. Oh, Lee Roy can talk to anyone! We love that about him. And his hilarious stories are endlessly entertaining. Well . . . not *endlessly*, but certainly entertaining.

I think I've just learned a lesson about days off on the road: You have only one per week, and sometimes the brain, as well as the body, needs to rest.

Still, I bought a bow tie. And we had some pie.

As our Seattle stay drew to an end, it finally rained, for several days straight. And that was so beautiful. It should rain in Seattle. It's only right— no matter what the locals say. I was beginning to feel gypped. A visit to Seattle without seeing any rain would have been like visiting France and not seeing any rude chain smokers having wine and cheese at a sidewalk café, reading Victor Hugo. It was still raining when we checked out of our hotel and climbed aboard the bus. Then, it was off to Portland, which, coincidentally, is the name of another step.

Nah. I'm kidding.

More to come, friends. Stay tuned.
Kostroff

10

PORTLAND FROM A HOTEL WINDOW

March 4th, 2003

"Michael Kostroff: Very, very talented. (Demons.)"
—*From an e-mail to Fred Applegate in which a friend, upon learning
that Fred had been cast in the first national tour of* The
Producers, *went through the cast list, giving brief descriptions of
each of Fred's future coworkers, based on their reputations.*

After only two weeks in Seattle, we were on the road again, this time by
bus, to Portland, where we were again booked for only two weeks. By now,
I was getting damned road weary, more so because of these shorter stops.
We arrived in town and dispersed to our various hotels.

Now, here's how the hotel thing works with professional touring shows like
ours: In each city, the company managers arrange discounted rates with a few
local hotels. They list these options for us, and they're what's called "company
housing." The company is responsible for transporting us to and from company housing. So they'll drop us off there upon arrival, get us to and from the
theatre, and pick us up there at the end of the run. It's convenient.

Of course, since we pay for our own lodging, we can stay wherever we want. Some stay with friends. Some try to find better deals at other places. But if you go outside the fold, you're on your own as far as transportation, dealing with the hotel, and so on.

Housing choices become very important when you live on the road, because your hotel room is your home for the time you're there. We don't just visit. We move in. And everyone has different criteria. For some, saving money is the highest priority. Those folks often choose the cheapest hotels and share with fellow cast members. For others, it's luxury, and cost be damned. For others, proximity to local activities is the thing. For me, the highest priority is a non-depressing atmosphere. Among other things, I need light. A view also helps a lot. And if the hotel room windows can be opened, allowing in some real, non-conditioned air, that's a huge plus. Cheap and funky? Fantastic! Cheap and sad? Not so good.

For the Portland run, I'd decided, for reasons that to this day remain shrouded in mystery, to go independent and book a room at the Clark Webster. One of our cast members had found the place on his own, and it sounded interesting: an older hotel in a cool neighborhood. To be honest, I hadn't really thought it through.

So, after the bus dropped us off, I had an additional schlep ahead of me to get to my chosen accommodations. It was raining. I called a cab, and waited in the warm, inviting, soft yellow lobby of the Marriott Hotel where fellow cast members were checking in, unpacking, taking hot showers, and, no doubt, eating bonbons in bed by now.

The cab dropped me off at the Clark Webster. It looked seedy and sad. Nevertheless, I pulled my suitcase up the wet steps to the lobby and checked in. Moments later, I threw open the door to my room and involuntarily muttered one little word that said it all:

"Nnnnnnnope."

What I saw was a tiny, dark, one-room flophouse flat. Old brown linoleum led to dingy carpeting beneath sad, cheap furnishings. There was a hollow wooden door to the coffin-sized bathroom, a slanted table and chairs, and a worn, olive-green knit blanket draped over a slightly sagging bed, which faced the ugly kitchenette on the opposite wall. The burners were rusty. The small refrigerator was dented. This room had one last chance at redemption. Was there a view? I shlumped skeptically over to the window and threw open the curtains. The window faced a brick wall.

I can't do it, I thought. Not now, when I'm feeling so over it, going loopy from the repetition and the travel and the physical exertion. I can't come back here every night, to the Despair Suite at Skid Row Manor, located at the corner of Hopeless and Loser. Nnnnnnnope.

Still in my coat, with my suitcase standing in the open door, I used the room phone to call our company manager. "Mark? Are there still rooms available at the Marriott?"

I hung up the phone, tugged my bags back downstairs, checked out, and got into another cab.

"Okay," I thought as I rode back, the day now nearly gone. "You're tired. You're wet. This isn't the highlight of the tour for you. This is one of those times when it's a job. Look, it's Portland. And we're only here for two weeks. So here's what you're going to do: Indulge. For the next two weeks, there are no judgments. Eat what you want, sleep all you want, and do whatever is soothing. You don't want to see the sights? Don't see 'em. You want room service? Order it. That's what a per diem is for. You're two cities away from home. Just do your job, collect the paycheck, and get through this slump."

The Marriott's front-desk staff was warm and helpful. It was almost as if they could sense my burnout. They gave me a room with a balcony and a view of the water. I don't know what body of water it was, because I never bothered to learn anything about Portland, except which floor the pool was on and how to get to the theatre. I checked in and came back down to the lobby, where I ran into a group of friends from the show, all cheery and laughing. I love show folk. There's always a hug and a laugh to be had. It was a relief to be back among them, no longer a renegade. Sometimes, there's something to be said for going with the crowd. They insisted I join them for dinner, and Fred and Michael invited me for a pre-dinner drink. "Gentlemen," I announced, lifting a much needed Margarita, "I hereby dub Portland 'City of Indulgence.'"

"Hear, hear," they agreed. (Hey, these guys will go along with anything.) Then I regaled them with my tale of the day's ordeal, which called for another round.

True to my temporary philosophy, I spent a lot of time in my room over the next two weeks. Really pulled a Howard Hughes and hid from the world most of the time. From my window, I could see ducks scurrying across the grass by the water. I watched boats sailing by. Watched cars cross the bridge. Occasionally, I saw the drawbridge lift to allow a tall boat to pass through. And that was excitement. I watched rain and sunsets, and sometimes, just sat and watched nothing. My very own three-star asylum.

I slept a lot. I felt no need to explore. I ordered room service, or ate at the hotel restaurant. I swam in the hotel pool. In the evening, I strolled to the theatre, just a few blocks away, did the show, and then went quietly back to my room. It was nice, really. Whenever I started to worry about this reclusive, inactive pattern, I reminded myself that it was just for this two-week period. No judgments.

This plan worked like gangbusters, and I started to enjoy my shameless laziness. "Laziness"—hah! I was still singing and dancing, climbing into and out of clothes all night as I performed my twelve roles. And when I thought about it, I decided that sometimes, doing the show is enough.

Now, staying at the same hotel with us was some sort of ladies' group. They were having a convention for their organization, which had a name like "Clovers and Rainbows" or "Daisies and Unicorns" or something like that. They all wore cutesy sweaters—you know, the kind with zigzags or pom-poms or stitched-on patterns of balloons or panda bears or kittens with big eyes. Their colorful nametags identified most of them as Trixie, Sandie, Barbie, Janie, Patsy, or Mitzi, and the rest as Carol. And these "Butterflies and Sprinkles" people were everywhere. Whenever I'd get on an elevator, there was another group of them, standing there, giggling. Oh, these girls were big gigglers. Nothing could possibly have been that funny.

These folks had a favorite line they liked to say: "Must have caught the local." Here's how it works: Whenever the elevator would make more than one stop, one of the "Happiness and Sunshine"-ers would chirp, "Oops! Must have caught the local!" and the elevator would erupt into a roar of giggles. They couldn't get enough of this clever quip. "Oops! Must have caught the local" was the surefire laugh-getter of the week. And each time, it got just as big a response, as if no one had ever made this clever observation before. "Oops! Must have caught the local" *killed* every time. And the reciter of the line was so admired by her colleagues for her outrageous wit that the giggles were inevitably followed by:

"Oh, she's a crazy one."

"Gotta watch out for her!"

"Didja start drinking early, Patsy?"

"We got our own stand-up comedian here!" . . . and then a round of sighs. Apparently, being a "Sparkles and Horsies" person (hell, I can't remember the damned name) filled one with an unjustifiable sense of fun.

And there I was, friends, Mr. I'm-From-New-York-And-I'm-Not-Amused. The jaded professional stage actor, dressed entirely in black, with a scarf around my neck to preserve my "instrument," glowering silently at the silly commoners. In my mind, I had a top hat, spats, a silver-tipped walking stick, a fur lined overcoat, and a stuck-up English accent. "Ladies," I imagined myself saying, "I am *in* comedy, and please trust me, none of you is the least bit funny."

Now, if you know me, you know that, as a rule, I'm not fond of chronic gigglers to begin with. But I'm even less enchanted when it's 7:15 PM and I'm trying to reach the theatre in time for the half-hour call, and I can't even get to the lobby because every elevator that comes along is crammed to capacity with gals in sweaters "taking the local" as I stand there smoldering, waiting for the next one . . . and the next . . . and the next . . . listening to the fading sound of distant giggles as each elevator continues to the floors below without me. Over and over, the same tease: the promising ding, the doors sliding open, wall-to-wall sweaters, and then, from somewhere within: "Oops! Must have caught the local," then the explosion of cackles as the doors slid closed again. I don't know what that organization does exactly (other than wear sweaters and ride elevators), but they sure had a lot of members. Or maybe the sweaters just took up a lot of room. Either way, it was hard to get to work.

And then, halfway through the Portland run, about the time that the "Angels and Froggies," mercifully, checked out, something unexpected happened that made me glad for my week of restful seclusion. Lewis, our star, called in sick one Friday night, and ended up being out for the entire five-show weekend. After months on the road, this man, who has the constitution of a train, just shut down for a few days. It was amazing that it hadn't happened sooner.

So I did five performances as Max in three days, back-to-back. Having been on several times before, I felt relatively comfortable in the part. But the five-show Max weekend is a marathon, requiring every ounce of available energy. There's no drinking and no talking, and you go right to bed after the show. Suddenly, having moved closer to the theatre and recharged my batteries by laying low seemed like brilliant foresight on my part. And I must confess, I'm beginning to love being called upon to play Max. I love how the company trusts me, and that the show goes on, even when we're missing our formidable lead. I love being the hero. And *man*, is the role fun! Completely exhausting, but fun.

But more importantly, all this provided a huge change in my routine, jostling me out of my ennui, sort of the way a trip to Mars strapped to a rocket might. It sounds strange, but my energetically demanding weekend as Max proved refreshing! At least it was different.

Here's the reality: Being on the road isn't always easy, and it isn't always fun. Sometimes you lose perspective. Sometimes you feel lost, like you're floating through space without an anchor, hurtling through the world without brakes. And sometimes, you just have to recharge. But even with the ups and downs, this is a great job. Eight times a week, we get to entertain thousands of people. It's a job I dreamed of. One which I'm fortunate to have. And it also bears mentioning (lest we forget) that it beats the hell out of waiting tables. I certainly did enough of that to really appreciate where I am today.

So, having successfully managed my bad mood, and having successfully conquered that dreaded beast known as the Five-Show Max, I was feeling rather restored as we left Portland.

San Francisco would be a nice long stop—eight weeks. So we'd get to settle in, put away our trunks, and get to know the city. It would be nice to have the same theatre, same dresser, and same home for a while.

On the morning we left, I took a long last look through the balcony window that had kept me calm and entertained for two weeks—the view that had been my therapy. Ducks were swimming. People were strolling. Boats were sailing. And a serene smirk crossed my face as I remembered that I'd moved to company housing, and the bus to the airport would be pulling right up to my hotel. Things were definitely looking up.

Photo: Robert Krueger.

Kostroff

11

CLANG, CLANG, CLANG WENT THE TROLLEY. POP, POP, POP WENT THE GASTROCNEMIUS

April 26th, 2003

Dear friends,

I wish you could see my face right now. I look like I'm about eight years old. Grinning like an idiot. I look like the family dog when he hangs his head out of the car window and squints in the wind. That's me. I'm riding on a cable car, which—I'm sorry, I don't care what anyone says—is cool. Now, there are three places for passengers to ride on a cable car. There's the rear section, which is enclosed, with benches along the sides that face in. Then there's the outside section, where the driver works, pulling and releasing the brakes. Here there are more benches, facing out. And then, beyond these benches—on the outside of the car—are the running boards, where passengers can stand, holding onto poles. That's where you want to be, especially if you're a boy. Because it's cool, and (you can pretend), dangerous. You're outside the car, on the edge, where it's exciting. You can feel the wind on your face. When the car climbs a steep hill, you really have to hang on tight. And when it slowly crests the top of that hill, and suddenly the boats on the sparkling bay or the shimmering buildings of downtown rise into view, it's really hard not to grin.

But what makes it even better . . . This is how I get to work every day! I'm not just some tourist. I'm a citizen! I throw on my neato *Producers* jacket, stroll down to my cable car stop, flash my monthly pass, thank you, and off I go to the theatre. I've acclimated so quickly, in fact, that I some-times find myself getting impatient with the visiting yokels who haven't yet grasped our transportation system. "C'mon people. Some of us have to get to work," I think, feigning annoyance. It's downright joyous.

You can always spot the tourists. They're the ones without jackets and hats. As we San Franciscans know, you always need a jacket and a hat, even on warmer days, because the temperature will plummet after dark. Supposedly, Mark Twain once wrote: "The coldest winter I ever saw was the summer I spent in San Francisco."* Oh, that Mark.

Unlike in Portland, where I hid inside for two weeks, here in San Francisco I've really been getting out and around and exploring. The other day, a tourist asked me for directions, and before I could say, "Sorry, I don't live here," I realized that I actually knew the answer. "Oh, you'll want to take the F train. It runs along Market. Or you can go down these stairs to the Metro . . . " Well, look at me. Just another helpful San Franciscan.

I'm sharing an apartment with a friend of a friend who lives here in Nob Hill, which, I've discovered, is the upscale neighborhood. I figured this out because whenever I mentioned I was living there, the reaction was: "Ohhh, excuse meee! Nob Hillll!" Scott, my host and roommate, works for Pottery Barn. You know when you leaf through those catalogues, how they have photos of these perfectly furnished rooms where everything matches

---

* *Unverified, though often attributed, according to* www.twainquotes.com.

and everything has its impossibly perfect place, and you think, "Who lives like this?" Well . . . this guy does. I mean, there's a color scheme, for goodness' sake. The candles are coordinated with the rooms. Every surface has two or three perfectly selected tchotchkes. If there were a magazine called *Apartment Beautiful,* this place would be in it.

It's a sweet, comfortable two-bedroom in a beautiful, old building with bay windows. Sunlight streams into my bedroom all day long. Scott works long hours on the weekdays, and I work most nights, so we hardly ever cross paths. Every once in a while he'll be up late after I get home from the theatre and we'll check in. I keep the cupboards and refrigerator stocked for myself so I can cook at home, listening to Ella Fitzgerald and Louis Armstrong on the living room stereo. I've called the phone company and activated the second phone line, in my room. The whole thing feels very much like I've moved to San Francisco.

We're right on the cable car line, and late at night, as I head to sleep, I can hear them going by. It's a lovely, spooky, comforting sound. It's hard to describe. A sort of scraping, but a pleasant scraping, like roller skates on pavement, only deeper, as it squeals to a stop. Then, in the nighttime silence, a bell, the signal that the car is about to resume its journey. It's romantic, and lonely, like the sound of a distant train in the middle of the night. You find yourself wondering who might be riding at that hour. I wish I could describe it better. It's a sound I've come to love. I'll miss it when the show moves on.

On our corner is a little hole-in-the-wall Chinese restaurant that just happens to be credited with having the best dumplings in the city. Oh, trust me, they're fantastic. Down another block is an unassuming little corner deli where they make great breakfasts on a hot plate behind the counter. It's become my regular haunt on matinee days.

To say that San Francisco is a great city is like saying that New York is a great city. Duh. No kidding. Many great writers have paid it tribute, and their observations are far more interesting than anything I could offer. So I'm not going to try to sum up San Francisco based on my little experience here. But I will say this: It's easy to see why hippies, poets, psychics, performance artists, experimental hallucinators, and other free thinkers have always gravitated toward this place. The light is different. It has a sunny haze that's utterly pixilating. Makes you feel trippy and groovy.

So, you've no doubt picked up a change in tone. Yes, I'm happy here. Hard not to be. It's a happy town. And I have my little routines, and the show is fun again, and, since the seven-month LA run is next, I've seen my last hotel for a while. I like hotels, but a steady diet of polyester bedspreads and the ding of elevators can get to you after a while. I'm enjoying the change.

The audiences are sharp here, and the show's getting a fine reception, though we've made an amusing discovery: When we play more conservative cities, they laugh louder. They have no problem with humor about Jews, gays, blacks, women, or anyone else. If it's funny, they laugh. But when we play the more liberal cities, they're not quite sure if it's okay to laugh at some of the jokes. It may not be correct. So they're a bit restrained. "Go figure!" one actor observed. "The liberals are conservative!"

And when it came to the show's "gay scene," in which we meet Roger, Carmen, and a houseful of very gay assistants—a scene which elicited *screams* all across the country—the San Francisco reaction seems to say "Yeah? So what? We see drag queens and leather men every day."

I have a few great friends here, one of whom I'd completely lost touch with. Then one night, there were Rebecca and her husband, waiting for me outside the stage door, wearing huge, matching smiles. They were as shocked and delighted to see me onstage as I was to see them afterwards. This is one of the perks of the road: surprise reunions. My friend Sue came out to visit her sister who lives here, and the three of us spent a fun day together being tourists. We watched sea lions, took the ferry to Sausalito, and ate dinner in Chinatown. Naturally, as a resident, I knew how to get to all those places.

In anticipation of our LA run, I decided to put together a "Kostroff Guide to Los Angeles," containing miscellaneous recommendations for restaurants, doctors, movie theatres, sightseeing, discounts, and so on, interspersed with jokes, insider tips, and driving shortcuts. Most of our company is out of New York, so I figured I'd help them get adjusted. It made for a fun project, and I'm very pleased with the result–sixteen pages' worth! The company managers copied and distributed "The Kostroff Guide" to the various dressing rooms the other day, and already I can hear people enjoying it, especially the jokes. Here's my favorite:

A Hollywood film director goes to heaven. St. Peter greets him at the gate.
St. Peter: Congratulations! You made it! By the way, God loves your work.
Director: Really? Wow. I didn't even know He liked the movies.
St. Peter: Oh, yes. In fact, now that you're here, God has chosen you to direct the greatest film of all time. We have Michelangelo to do the sets, da Vinci for special effects, and Monet designing the costumes. The script is by Shakespeare, the score is by Bach, we have Billie Holiday to sing the main theme, and it's going to star Olivier, Barrymore, Bernhardt–the greatest actors of all time.
Director: Wow. It's the perfect movie! So, who's the leading lady?
St. Peter: Yeah . . . Well, scc, that's the thing.
Director: What?
St. Peter: You see, God has this girlfriend . . .

We're approaching the "Changing of the Guard," when Jason Alexander and Martin Short will take over for Lewis and Don. The two "names" will join us here in San Francisco for daytime rehearsals as we continue to perform the show at night with the current cast, and then the producers have decided to "sneak" them into the show, unannounced, for the final week of the San Francisco run–a dress rehearsal for them, and a great surprise for the audiences!

Once we get to LA, the "Great Juggle" takes place: Jason and Martin officially take over the leads. Lewis and Don go to Broadway. The *current*

Broadway leads leave to star in the second national tour. Lee Roy *also* goes to the second national tour, replaced in our company by Gary Beach. Josh Prince replaces Michael Paternostro, and Michael leaves the show altogether, having decided not to continue to LA. Complicated, I know. Even we have a hard time keeping track.

It's a weird time. As much as we look forward to working with our new guys, we've been through quite a journey with Lewis, Don, Lee Roy, and Michael. And, though they may return after LA, we all know the show's about to change substantially. It's the end of an era.

And then it got even weirder, when Michael broke his foot and had to leave us early. It was an abrupt good-bye to a guy who's been a terrific asset to the company, in both personality and talent. Josh will step in earlier than planned.

Meanwhile, as my agent Eric would say, "Here's something interesting . . ."

Lewis Stadlen will be taking a week's vacation before going to Broadway, which leaves a one-week gap before Jason goes on in San Francisco. So I have an exciting opportunity. I'll be playing Max for an entire week while everyone is here: Mel Brooks, Susan Stroman, Jason, Martin, and several of the producers. None of these folks have seen me in the role, so it's good for my future with the show. Apparently they've heard good things, and they all want to see me. I think they're grooming me as a future Max.

Our new stars arrived on a Thursday, and we began rehearsals. It was great to see Jason, who's a friend. We'd worked together years ago, and I found him to be among the warmest, realest, most genuinely nice guys you could ever hope to meet. We've stayed in touch over the years, and we've been greatly looking forward to working together again.

That night, we did our show. It was an exciting evening, knowing everyone was there. It was the first time Ms. Stroman had seen us since we opened in Pittsburgh last September. We knew the show was good, and we wanted her to see that. And, we knew it was one of our last shows with Lewis and Don and Lee Roy, who were as funny as ever. As always, the audience howled.

I suppose, if anything, I may have been doing things with more gusto than usual. Or maybe there was some subconscious self-sabotage. Who knows? All I can tell you is that, minutes into Act Two, I was running off into the wings when I felt a small pop and a tingle in my left calf. Nothing terribly painful. Could have been a cramp . . . But it wasn't.

I limped offstage. Rolt rushed over.

"Can you go on?"

"I . . . I don't know . . ."

"Try walking."

"Okay." *(I hobble a few steps.)*

"How does it feel? Should we put Goddard on?"

"I . . . I don't know."

"Michael, we have to make a decision. Put it this way: Can you tap?"

Me: *(laughing)* "Hahahaha . . . no."

And that was that. Goddard (on a moment's notice) suited up and finished the show in my place. I limped to the dressing room alone, iced the injury, changed, and quietly went home while the show continued.

The next day, I went to the doctor. I was sure it was just a sprain or something. No such luck. I had torn my gastrocnemius—a calf muscle. Who knew? Funny how you always learn Latin when you injure yourself. All I wanted to know was how long it would be before I could return to the show. I was on as Max in just a few days. I knew Rolt would need information. The doctor wasn't sure. Three-to-ten days, maybe.

Now, ten days would mean missing my big chance to play Max for the bigwigs. So I decided it would be three.

But doctors, my friend Mary will tell you, always lie. Always. They say a week, it's a month. They say six weeks, it's eight. In this case, they kept extending the estimate. "I don't know why the doctor said three-to-ten days," the physical therapist told me a few days later. "Injuries like this always take fourteen days, minimum." (And even that, it turned out, was a lie.) My three-day plan was out the window. I couldn't manage to walk in a manner that resembled that of a human person. Secretly, I tried a dance step or two back at the apartment. It looked like I was sneaking barefoot across hot coals. And no one wants to see that. This was going to take a while.

The following week, Fred Applegate went on as Max in my place, and everyone was very pleased. I hopped (literally) into a cab and headed down to the theatre to see his first performance and I must say, it was thrilling. He saved the day, as I'd done back in Cleveland. Knowing the part as well as I do, I knew what a big feat that was. Herculean! And I was so proud of him. So was everyone else, including Brooks and Stroman.

I ran into Ms. Stroman backstage at intermission. "I'm sorry you didn't get to see me do Max," I shrugged sheepishly. "What can I tell you? It's the key to comedy: timing."

Yes. Timing. Let's talk timing.

I began to amuse myself thinking of all the better times this could have happened. If I had to injure myself and be out of the show, why couldn't it have happened in Cleveland? You all remember Cleveland, where I hated the city and my job but loved my apartment? That would have been a perfect time to tear the ol' gastrocnemius. Or how about Portland? I was hibernating there anyway. I could have convalesced by the pool while munching on room service cuisine. Or why not San Diego, where I was blissfully enjoying the heavenly weather and the great hotel? If it had happened there, I could have recuperated surrounded by kids and a dog at my friend Ame's house. Think of the sympathy! But noooooo. I had to go injure myself in a great city that I loved exploring, days before my first opportunity to play the lead in *The Producers* with everyone watching. Timing. Ba-dum-bum. Is this thing on?

And so, my friends, my life in San Francisco changed suddenly and drastically. The injury, while not especially painful, was especially annoying, particularly in a city made up of hills. Tearing your gastrocnemius affects your foot's range of motion, so it's painful to flex. Hills: bad. So, I sat at home at night while the show went on, cabbed to physical therapy several times a week, and fought boredom. I kept in touch with Rolt, keeping him apprised of the latest false estimate of when I'd be back in the show.

At first, I hung out at the theatre during the day, watching rehearsals, so I could feel like an involved member of the company. But after a while, I realized I was making people uncomfortable. They seemed to feel like they had to extend sympathy whenever they saw me. And I think that was getting old for all of us. I had to come to terms with the fact that, for the moment, I wasn't part of the show. In the grand tradition, it was going on without me.

So I watched TV, chatted online. To cheer myself up, I decided to plan my vacation, and that helped a bit. I wandered through hundreds of online photos of beautiful vacation spots in the sunny Mexican Caribbean in search of the locale that would most closely resemble those Corona beer commercials. Picturing myself there became my great pastime. Sometimes, I'd get ambitious and hop to the kitchen, or out to the stoop for some air. Taking a shower required circus skills. A few closer friends in the company checked up on me once or twice. I put on a cheery voice, cracked a few jokes, but it was lonely. I felt forgotten.

I listened to the cable car ring its bell late at night. I missed riding on them.

I don't remember much about San Francisco after that. I suppose I could have gone home to LA, but the doctors were still stringing me along, and I wanted to return to work as soon as I could. "Maybe another week or two," they were now telling me.

"But you said three weeks, tops!"

"Three weeks?! Oh, no. These things are *always* four weeks, minimum." Liars.

All in all, it really wasn't a tragedy. Just an inconvenience, a disappointment, and a big drag. People love to try to think of reasons why things happen as they do. I have a different kind of philosophy. It goes like this: Some things just suck. Shit happens. No point in making yourself crazy wondering why. There isn't always a reason. And I was lucky. At least I had a job to go back to, which, among other things, provided tremendous incentive. I couldn't *wait* to get back to work, and that made me a model physical therapy patient.

And as the run drew to a close back at the theatre, I was at home in my Pottery Barn bedroom, packing my trunk, happily anticipating being back in my own apartment. I was getting around fairly well by now, and I greatly looked forward to returning to the show in time for the LA previews. But now, as I contemplated going back on the stage again, a new concern arose . . .

After a month's absence, would I remember my roles?

There was one thing I knew for sure. I never again wanted to hear someone wish me "break a leg."

Stay tuned, readers.

Kostroff

12

THE END OF THE ROAD
(OR "NEVER SAY NEVER AGAIN")

September 1st, 2003

The cast of the first national tour of *The Producers* arrived in Los Angeles much as we had in other cities—a lively, bustling gaggle of chattering show folk in hats and jackets bearing the show's logo, hovering around a luggage carousel in a baggage claim area at yet another airport, some on cell phones, checking in with local friends, some reassuring their confused pets, some hauling bags off the carousel, some chatting with each other, and our company manager, Mark, overseeing the whole transition.

Waiting off to the side, I found myself next to a friendly guy with a clipboard, who struck up a conversation.

"So, you all with *The Producers*?"

"Yeah."

"Cool. I hear that's good."

"Oh, it is. Very funny show."

"Yeah, I'm just here organizing a tour. Actually, I'm never here. This is just a part-time thing. I'm a screenwriter. In fact I had a reading of one of my screenplays last week. Lot of interest. This guy from Sony . . . "

And as he continued, a smirk crept across my face. Yep. No question. We'd definitely landed in LA.

Since the show is sitting down here for more than seven months, and because LA is so big, the group dynamics would be very different here as we splintered off in our various directions from the airport. Some already live here, so they went home to their respective houses, spouses, and kids. Some had found sublets just for the run. Some opted for hotel rooms. And one even bought a house with his partner, who packed up the dogs and relocated from New York.

And after everyone had dispersed, I found myself sitting once again in my very own living room. And suddenly, I wasn't on tour anymore. I blinked. Did all that really happen? What had, at times, felt like an eternity on the road now felt like about a week. There I was, with my old familiar couch, my TV, my stuff, my walls, my neighbors, my mailbox. Familiar sounds. I hauled boxes out of the garage and started putting things away, wondering if I'd dreamed the whole thing.

Now, at some point—I don't know when—I'd made a decision not to continue with the show after its LA run. It was time for new adventures, I needed to get back to cultivating my TV career and, while it had certainly been a fascinating and fun trip, after nearly a year, I'd had enough with the traveling already. So now, I was off the road for good. And that was a strange thing to take in.

I loved being back, not having the stress of finding things like drug stores and dry cleaners. I shopped in my old familiar supermarket and cooked in my own kitchen and saw friends I hadn't seen in a year.

And I was able to return to one of my favorite hobbies, skewering the city in which I live.

Now, Los Angeles, for those of you who've never visited, functions in a unique and rather cockeyed manner. Scientists have pondered it for years. Maybe it's something in the bottled water.

For one thing, every single resident, from Pasadena to Malibu, is either an actor or a writer—even if he's never trained or worked in those fields, and even if there's no evidence of any talent whatsoever. He merely dubs himself an actor or a writer and waits for the calls to start coming in. Also, everyone has a cell phone. I believe there's a law or something. That's because everyone here is, or aspires to be, Important. Being Important, in fact, is what LA life is all about. If you're not Important, or right on the brink of Important, you might as well move. And so the Important people talk Importantly on their cell phones all day long, discussing, in public, very Important things, like their current weight (and when I say current, I mean their weight at that very moment), the latest episode of their favorite reality television program, or how stupid other people are. These are calls that can't wait.

Occasionally, Los Angeles drivers are either dumb or hostile. But more often, they're both. New York drivers will honk and give you the finger if you do something stupid while driving. LA drivers will honk and give you the finger if *they've* done something stupid while driving.

It's interesting to note that there are no great songs written about LA. That's because, to quote Gertrude Stein, "There is no *there* there." The one song that comes to mind, Randy Newman's "I Love LA," is a mockery of the shallow lifestyle, but most of the natives missed that. In fact, a few years back, there was a movement to make it the city's official theme song.

Here, friends make plans, and then those plans simply don't take place. Because there's an unwritten understanding that all commitments are theoretical. This is what's referred to, in the local parlance, as "penciling it in"—a euphemism for making plans that both parties agree to ignore once they're made. This is done so that the participants can decline other offers because they now "have plans."

In fact, many things mean other things here, which is why I included this brief LA-to-English dictionary as part of my "Kostroff Guide to Los Angeles":

I'll call you tomorrow: You may or may not hear from me some time within the next two weeks, depending on whether or not you can do anything for me.

You were great in the show: Do you know anyone Important?

What have you done?: Forget all this theatre, do you have any *real* credits?

Let's get together some time: Get lost.

No, really. Let's get together some time: Okay, call me, but don't expect me to remember you.

I'll meet you there at 7: If I remember to show up, it'll be around 7:45, but I may find something better to do.

Dude, what's your deal?: Why are you so uptight about me being a flake?

These bagels taste just like New York bagels!: I have never been to New York.

cold: Less than sixty degrees Fahrenheit.

You're so New York: I find you pushy and demanding, and you walk too fast.

Okay, so I pick on LA. I don't mean any offense. After all, I've chosen to live here for the past fourteen years. But for New Yorkers, LA bashing is a pastime. In fact, some of us view it as an obligation. I'm just being true to my roots.

The Pantages Theatre in Hollywood had been decked out like no other theatre we'd played. Enormous billboards along the top of the building displayed supersized Jason Alexanders and Martin Shorts in various poses. And at the corner, our glittering gold showgirls smiled, beguiling all of Hollywood Boulevard. At the backstage entrance, velvet ropes were set up to keep the autograph seekers at bay. It was a new era.

As we got into previews, the response was just as we'd expected: through the roof. Not only because the show is so good, which it is, but also because LA audiences love anything that features "name" actors. "Hey! I know that guy from TV! This must be good!" (It's the reason I'm predicting Arnold Schwarzenegger will be successful in his run for governor.*)

As for the rest of us, well, we knew we were now in a star vehicle, and that was just fine, especially because Jason and Martin are terrifically talented and absolutely lovely guys. The enthusiastic response was well deserved. Besides, I'm happy when an audience enjoys a show, regardless of the reason. Still, as our Nazi Tenor, Daniel Heron, observed, "We could be standing out there naked, and these folks would say 'Oh, look at the hilarious way Jason and Martin are reacting to those naked people.'"

Opening night was to be a huge event: TV cameras, celebrities, klieg lights. In fact, they closed off several streets for the occasion. There would be a red carpet, leading from the theatre all the way down Argyle Street to the Palladium, where the opening night party was to be held. A shuttle would run back and forth. A special map and instructions were issued. I've never been involved in anything this glamorous. The cast planned their dressy outfits with the greatest of care. (Mine was decidedly Daddio Visits the Studio, down to my black-and-white wingtips, Jack. Snazz-a-palooza!)

"Kids," I told my cast mates, "mark my words: It ain't our night. It's all about Jason, Martin, Susan, and Mel." I joked that we should have buttons made for ourselves that read, "YES, I'M IN THE SHOW," since no one was going to recognize us.

On the big night, we all arrived at the theatre with our garment bags (and whatever additional paraphernalia comes out of all those sexy little zip-up, snap-shut cases and silky bags that women always tote along in preparation for such events. Like most men, I'm completely in the dark about what actually happens in that intriguing process, but the results are stunning. Part of The Feminine Mystique.) The place was a scene. As we slipped invisibly into the stage entrance around the corner, Hollywood Boulevard was abuzz with activity. "Handlers" with walkie-talkies directed

*Nyah, nyah. I was right.

guests to the appropriate spots to collect their tickets and their VIP party passes. There was an *Entertainment Tonight* backdrop set up for interviews with celebrity guests. Limos vied for curb space to drop off their well-heeled passengers. Klieg lights ballyhooed across the smoggy sky.

The show was received with fantastic enthusiasm. Every joke landed. Every number wowed 'em. It was a triumphant night for all of us. And it was great to show off the results of many months of honing our performances on the road. LA loved us!

As soon as the show came down*, everyone hit the showers. I'd agreed to wait for the character women, Jessica, Pam, and Nancy. It took a while for them to complete all their mysterious female magic tricks, but you can't rush perfection. So I waited, all dolled up, in the hallway. When they finally emerged from the dressing room, they looked fantastic! Three visions in satin and chiffon. Together, we looked like a sleazy Italian gold digger escorting rich American heiresses to a high society gala.

And so we emerged into the warm May night, ready to shield our eyes from the flurry of flashbulbs and competing paparazzi, only to find . . . an empty street, covered by a long red carpet, with no one on it. Everything was quiet. The Important people were already at the party. We didn't care. We looked gorgeous, even if no one saw us as we strolled the two blocks to Sunset Boulevard and entered the Palladium.

The place was beautiful. Long swaths of white fabric draped everything. There was a live band, a beautiful buffet, and people everywhere. The guest list was impressive: Steven Spielberg, Larry King, Alec Baldwin, Tim Allen, Tom Hanks and Rita Wilson, Christopher Guest and Jamie Lee Curtis, Carl Reiner, Rob Reiner, Sally Field, Garry Shandling, Catherine O'Hara, Goldie Hawn, Billy Crystal, Mo Gaffney, Richard Lewis, Dennis Miller, Cloris Leachman, Andrea Martin, Jon Lovitz, Carol Burnett, Larry David, Garry Marshall, Doris Roberts, Kate Hudson, Julia Louis-Dreyfus, Joely Fisher, Betty White, Neil Patrick Harris, David Hasselhoff, Red Buttons, Eugene

---

came down: Ended, in theatre jargon.

Levy, Mr. Blackwell, Tracey Ullman, and of course, our Mrs. Brooks, Anne Bancroft, all there, in person, to see our show.

Jason, Martin, and Mel were each trapped deep within three respective mobs of reporters and celebrity well-wishers, where lights, cameras, and microphones competed for access. The rest of us noshed and hung out with our guests, anonymously. There was a strange and awkward moment when Susan Stroman walked onto the bandstand and announced, over the clatter and chatter, "Ladies and gentlemen, I'd like to present the cast of *The Producers.*" We didn't know if we were supposed to come up or wave or what. But no one stopped eating or talking, so she quietly left the stage as the band started another number. Apparently, it wasn't even her night. And she *created* the thing. Very strange town.

The highlight for me was running into a substantial number of friends and former associates–people with whom I'd done theme park shows and regional theatre, "blue-collar" actors like me. They were so proud and excited to see me in such a big production. And that made my night. Only folks who know where you've come from can truly appreciate your accomplishments.

With opening night behind us, we settled into our run. It was mostly uneventful, and that wasn't a bad thing at all. In fact, we all enjoyed the routine. We went to work, did our "little skit," and went home. I puttered contentedly around my apartment. It was a nice, even-keel kind of time. Jason Alexander and Martin Short are constant delights to work with. Jason–for whom the word "mensch"* was invented–is the dearest, warmest guy in show business. And Martin, well, he's a maniac, always trying to make us break onstage, often successfully. He cracks up Jason nearly every night.

Now, I don't usually look at the audience much. But some of my onstage associates have perfected the art of surreptitiously assessing our patrons. They'll sneak looks and compare notes on who's cute, who looks bored, who's dressed funny, etc. (The only thing that always seems to catch my eye is when someone arrives late, or leaves during the curtain call–two pet

*mensch: (Yiddish) A fine, kind-hearted, upstanding man.

peeves of mine.) Anyway, one night, we're in the middle of the big "King of Broadway" number when I notice several of my pals quaking with suppressed laughter. Tears were streaming down cheeks as they tried to keep it together. "What's going on?" I whispered to Jessica as I danced near her.

"There's a whole row of people wearing surgical masks. Fifth row, left of center."

Now, here's how weak I am: I didn't even have to look. The mental image was enough to send me over the edge—did someone tell them that theatre air was unhealthy?—and I was gone too. And then, like an idiot, I *did* look . . .

Friends, I don't know who sang the chorus parts that night. It sure wasn't I. And I'm pretty sure that about half of the ensemble was rendered mute at that point as well. It was a stage full of shaking shoulders. Somehow, we got through the number, but I had to keep my eyes off the audience for the rest of the night . . . and think very sad, serious thoughts!

By late June, I'd adjusted my planned departure date. I'd decided that, rather than finish the LA run, I'd leave in September, our one-year mark. I *loved* doing *The Producers*, and greatly hoped to return at some point, but a year felt like the right amount of time for now. I was ready for a long rest from the eight-show-a-week schedule. I looked forward to spending a nice, quiet fall in LA, pursuing television roles—no singing, no dancing, no traveling. My nights free to hang out with friends. Easy. And once I'd made the decision, I started to get excited by the idea that the end was clearly in sight. Maybe I'd tour again in a few years. For now, I was happily resolved to stay put.

I was driving along Santa Monica Boulevard when my cell phone rang. (Yes. I have one. Okay, you got me.) The voice of Eric, my stage agent, piped through the tiny speaker:

"Now here's an interesting call I got today. *Les Misérables* wants to know if you'd like to go out on tour playing Thénardier. They don't need to audition you again. They just want to know if you'll do it."

Me: (*halfway through Eric's last sentence*) "Yep!"

You would think I would have thought about it for a moment before abruptly abandoning my well-made retirement plans. Weighed some pros and cons. Considered my options. But no. Because, friends—your narrator is, quite simply, a hopeless case. I love the theatre. And I mean . . . *Les Misérables*! How could I say no to such juicy role in such a terrific show?

Besides, since there would be no dancing and far fewer costume changes, it might be enough of a break from my strenuous, busy track in *The Producers*, I convinced myself.

A little background: I'd been in to audition for *Les Mis* five or six times over the years. They always said I was at the top of their list, but that neither of the actors playing the role (on Broadway or on tour) was leaving. When the part finally opened up—for the first time in about ten years—I was in rehearsals for *The Producers*, so I wasn't available. *This* time, they just offered me the job, and the timing was perfect for both of us.

So . . . I was leaving the show. And joining a new one. Just like that. I started re-boxing things I'd "de-boxed" just a few months earlier and returning them to the garage whence they came. Never a single doubt about my decision.

With just seven weeks remaining, I was particularly smug about the fact that I'd escaped ever having to go on as Roger De Bris, a role for which I was the second cover. I'd learned it, but I'd always been resistant. I just didn't feel I'd be any good in the part. It wasn't "me" the way that Max is. Fortunately, as second cover, I knew I'd never go on. Gary Beach rarely missed shows. And if he did, Kevin Ligon, the first cover, was there to fill in, and he was absolutely marvelous in the role.

And then, bizarrely, Kevin went out with the same exact injury I'd had—a torn calf muscle (extra credit if you can remember the Latin name for it). In fact, *both* of us had torn our *left* calf muscles, *both* on the Thursday before we were to go on in a principal role. (He was supposed to play Franz Liebkind all the following week, just as I'd been scheduled to play Max back in San Francisco.) Odd.

The implications didn't hit me until Rolt clapped his hand on my shoulder and said, "Now, Michael, just so you understand: With Kevin out, you're the man. If Gary goes out, you're on."

"Yeah, but Gary's not going out, is he?"

He smirked. "You never know." Rolt's been doing this a while, and knows that anything is possible.

Sure enough, he called a few days later to say that Gary Beach would be taking a day off in two weeks. Shit.

Now it was time to get very serious about Roger De Bris. Whatever resistance I'd had, it was time to get over it. I was going on. No way around it. I was called in for extra rehearsals, which I needed, and gave the part a lot more thought. The wardrobe supervisor taught me how to walk in the high heels and a $10,000 beaded gown that Roger wears in Act One. (Land and swoosh. That's the trick.) (. . . You know, in case any of you fellas ever need to walk in a $10,000 beaded gown.) By the night, I felt ready. I really wasn't looking forward to it, but I figured I'd just do my best, try not to let the show down, and then put it behind me.

Several friends had tickets for that night. I'd tried to talk them out of coming. "I've never played Roger before. It's not going to be good. Come back when I'm doing my usual parts!" They wouldn't listen to reason. One friend, who was dead broke, was so determined to see me go on that he bribed an usher and managed to get a seat at the last minute. *That's* a friend.

Technically, everything went fine. I remembered the lines, didn't trip on the dress, faked my way through the tap dancing, and found the lung capacity, somewhere, to get through the aerobic "Springtime for Hitler." And as always, the cast was generously supportive. But the huge surprise was this: I *loved* playing the part! I'd never been so wrong! My friends—it was great sharing my one-night-only performance as Roger with them—said I looked like I was having the time of my life. And I suppose they were right. Afterwards, I kind of wanted to do it again, though I knew that would never happen. Still, what a surprise to have a fun "last hurrah" so close to the end of my time with the show!

Are you detecting a pattern?

The following week, I was on again as Roger. Even more fun the second time. Jason and Martin were so comfortable, they started trying to crack me up onstage. Dear Kevin even showed up, limping, to cheer me on, just as I'd done with Fred when he debuted as Max. If "There's no people like show people" weren't such a horrible cliché (not to mention a grammatically incorrect one), I'd be tempted to use it here.

My last week with the show was bliss. As you've no doubt gleaned from these reports, there's a cycle to such things. Some nights, you want to burst out of your skin from the glorious, outrageous euphoria of it all. Other nights, it's like slogging through mud in a lead suit, carrying an anvil on your head. But that last

Goddard, going on as me while I play Roger.
Photo: Michael Thomas Holmes.

week, I felt light. Nothing hurt. My voice was healthy. I performed with abandon, and I relished every laugh. (*Les Mis* isn't exactly known for its zany hilarity and wacky antics, so I tried to store them up.)

The end was nice. I posted a good-bye note on the company callboard. It read:

Dear show biz friends,

When it comes to good-byes, I'm not particularly sentimental. We have so many of them in our profession—too many to get worked up over—and, happily, they're often soon followed by reunions.

But I do want to say, in parting—and I mean this—that it's been a privilege working with each and every one of you. And it's been an adventure as well. Together, we gave a lot of people a really funny fucking evening at the theatre. And that's something these days.

For those of you who'd like to stay in touch, I'd love an e-mail every now and again.

And there you have it. Off I go. Take care, everyone.

Kostroff

After my final curtain, this terrific company sang to me: *"Happy trails to you . . . until we meet again . . . Happy trails to you . . . keep smiling until then . . . "* and presented me with a super-duper space-age backpack; a card, signed by everyone, which applauds when you open it; and a copy of the complete, unabridged *Les Misérables!* Appropriately, there were no tears or attempts at closure, only hugs, pats on the back, and, "Seeya 'round, Kostroff." And that is as it should be, I believe. There's a good chance I'll find myself in some company of *The Producers* again at some later date, working with some of the same folks. And it'll be good to see them. Until then . . .

"Happy trails . . . to you . . . till we meet again."

The next morning, my alarm raised me at 6 AM. I'd been pretty much packed for the last week. Now it was time to go. I'd be flying to Atlanta, then starting rehearsals the very next day. There would be only two weeks before opening night—not much time to learn a whole new show. I could hardly wait to get to work . . .

Never say you're done with touring. You'll live to eat your words. Never say you'll never play Roger De Bris. Rest assured, sooner or later, you'll don the sequined dress—maybe even twice. Never say never. That's only one of the handful of lessons I've learned during my road experience of the past year. As I think about it, some others come to mind:

Pace yourself, find the mall, make friends with your dresser, don't be too intense, focus on the positive but don't freak out when you lose sight of it: It comes back. Cut yourself some slack; in fact, cut yourself lots of slack. See a movie, read a book, order room service, relax during the day when you feel like it (remember, you work a night shift), but see what's interesting and unique about each town when you can. Don't wait for people to invite you. Invite them. Go out of your way to compliment people when you like what they're doing. And as often as possible, find a way to remind yourself that people saved up their money, hired a sitter, and planned an evening around coming to the theatre and seeing your show. Give them the very, very best you have to give that night. Someone may be seeing his first show. Someone else may be seeing his last. It's when I lose that connection with the people in the seats that my efforts begin to feel futile. Each performance is a conversation. The audience is the silent half of that conversation. I mustn't forget that.

I think other lessons will only become clear with time and distance.

Finally, never say you're at "The End of the Road." As it turned out, in this case, the road was merely curving, and there would be more *Letters from Backstage* to be written.

Sit tight, everyone. Here we go again . . .
Kostroff

Illustration: Patrick Richwood.

13

REVOLUTIONS, FRENCH AND OTHERWISE

September 22nd, 2003

My eyes popped open. It was a Tuesday morning. I was in a hotel bed.

I stumbled to the window . . . pulled open the blinds. And I started to laugh. Another strange city. Where was I? What had I gone and done? Signed on for another tour. My God. What was I thinking? I was back out on the road. And it was too late to change my mind now.

And I got all happy inside. Outrageously, stupidly, gleefully happy, as a man does when he's playing hooky from the real world. A life lived in hotels, sleeping late, working nights, playing "make pretend" for a living was once again before me. And I felt like Huckleberry Finn, out on his raft on the great, wide Mississippi. Free. No walls. Drifting along . . . but with a nice weekly paycheck. I get a kick out of being 100 percent wrong about myself. I thought I'd had enough of touring. Who was I kidding? I love this stuff.

Only two days earlier, I'd been in Los Angeles, doing my last two-show Sunday with *The Producers* and saying my good-byes. On Monday, I got up at 6 AM and flew for most of the day, landing here, in Atlanta, in time for a late dinner at the hotel bar and my habitual stroll through the new neighborhood. The theatre marquee across the street spelled out "LES MISERABLES" in little bulbs, with an opening date that was way too soon to be accurate. I went back to my room, still in a bit of a fog, and crashed.

Now it was Tuesday morning, and with all the packing, good-byes, and jet lag behind me, it all felt real and clear for the first time. I was off on a new adventure.

A few hours later, fed and washed, I found myself standing inside Atlanta's Fox Theatre—another beautiful, ornate shrine, this one built to resemble the outdoor courtyard of a North African palace . . . but of course. (I later learned the formal name for the theatre's design style: "Neo–Middle Eastern Exotic.") This grand, elegant auditorium accommodated as many as 4,600 playgoers, and its décor was outrageous. A striped canopy resembling a nomad's tent extended from the back wall and out over the balcony. Above the stage hung a false stone bridge with Oriental rugs draped over its side, masking speakers. Follow spots stood like cannons along the tops of the castle walls. The ceiling was an endless night sky, with flickering stars, and dark clouds, which drifted subtly along, thanks to hidden lighting instruments.

Even the backstage was grand. There, I discovered seven floors of dressing rooms, accessed by one of those old elevators with a heavy, manually operated sliding gate. The basement, where wardrobe and hair had been situated, featured a labyrinth of corridors so complex and far-reaching that when the Metropolitan Opera played the Fox, they renamed each hallway after a New York street, so they wouldn't get lost.

But as transporting as all that was, I was even more mesmerized by what I saw on the stage of this beautiful old theatre: a familiar looking burnt-out nineteenth-century French city, being assembled by crew members in *Les Misérables* tee shirts. I'd seen this great, grand, classic musical several times over the years. What a remarkable circumstance it was to be a part of it. What a turn of events.

What had I gone and done?

Two weeks isn't much time to learn and rehearse a whole new show. But the easy, happy, creative tone set by our director, Jason Moore, and his production team, made it all happen without even a moment of anxiety. They've been doing this for a while.

The first rehearsal told me this was going to be a whole new world for me—vastly different from other experiences. As the company gathered in a circle, Jason explained his policy: Rather than asking new cast members to copy what their predecessors did, he encouraged them to really create and own their roles—even to make slightly different choices every night, as long they're faithful to the telling of the story. Blocking could change, but the story must be told. "Free *Les Mis*," they call it. Throughout rehearsals, he'd vividly flesh out what the times were like (France in the period following the French Revolution), what people's lives were like (the poverty, the injustice), and so on, often using Victor Hugo's novel for reference. Instead of working technically, he *infused* us with the show.

Similarly, the musical director, Dale, encouraged singing that was appropriate to both story and character, rather than simply pretty. The convicts in the chain gang, for example, who open the show, should be grunting as they work, not crooning.

These directions were vastly different from the precise, straight-line, pre-set, movement-based world of *The Producers*, where the scenes are literally staged "by the numbers." (Musicals often have numbers at the edge of the stage so dancers can space themselves evenly. In *The Producers*, we use these numbers for scenes as well: "Walk three steps to six, point your finger, and say the line over your left shoulder, looking towards eight. Then, when you say the word 'time,' move out to twelve.") This "Free *Les Mis*" approach was . . . revolutionary.

And speaking of revolutions: For the few of you who didn't know, *Les Misérables* is staged on a turntable that revolves throughout the show to indicate travel, the passage of time, or a change of location. It's a wonderfully effective staging technique . . . and a bitch to work on. At our third rehearsal, those of us who are new to the show spent about an hour learning how to get on and off the damned thing while it's moving, which was hilarious. Going from a nice, solid stationary floor onto this giant spinning disc is a truly odd sensation. We looked like a bunch of drunks taking a sobriety test . . . and failing. There is an actual technique, which I've yet to master. Even now, as we perform the show in front of an audience, I usually just do a little jeté* and hope for the best.

But that's just getting on and off. Getting used to the movement is another matter altogether. It's one of the unique things about this particular job. You'll be in the middle of a perfectly normal interaction with another character, when suddenly, the floor will start moving. It's the Mad Tea Party ride at Disneyland, if you had to stand and sing while riding it. For several nights, when I'd lie down to go to sleep after a day of rehearsal, I could still feel it turning, like when you come home from a day at the ocean and still feel the waves.

Stage directions, meanwhile, are nearly impossible to explain. "Okay," my poor stage manager began one day, his face full of earnest concentration. "At the end of this scene, you guys'll head off in the direction of what *would* be stage right . . . except you'll actually be exiting *left*, because the turntable will revolve and you'll end up there, so right . . . *becomes* . . . left."

* jeté: A ballet leap. Literally, it means "thrown."

Our eyes betrayed our total, absolute incomprehension as we stared at him like English wasn't our first language. He rubbed his face, frustrated at his inability to explain. "Okay. I think this will make more sense when we actually do it." And this kind of exchange happened daily, until it somehow became as normal as can be. In one scene, I begin a conversation with another character downstage center. He walks away, and I pursue him all the way upstage center. But by the time we get there, we're downstage center again! It's like being in an Escher painting, with people walking upstairs to the bottom of a building.

On top of that, the stage is "raked" (theatre terminology for a stage that's slanted toward the audience for better visibility). So we're slanted, we're turning, we don't know right from left, and we're singing. Welcome to my new gig.

But the most daunting part of my role is probably my big number, "Master of the House," in which my character, Thénardier, gleefully demonstrates the various ways he swindles the guests at his inn. While singing, I greet travelers, take orders, steal things, deliver asides to the audience, prepare imaginary food, interact with my partner in crime, Madame Thénardier (played by the delightful Cindy Benson), and lead the sing-along choruses. It's like a juggling act. Lots of words. Lots of business. And in the midst of all this, the stage turns whenever I go back and forth between the kitchen and the dining room. Boy, just when you think you're done waiting tables . . .

This tour is, technically, a new one. The show's producers had closed down the previous U.S. tour for a summer hiatus. When it was time to start up again, they decided to do some recasting. So they brought in some people from the recently closed Broadway company, some from the outside, who'd never done the show before (the "new-news," we're called), and some from the previous, pre-hiatus touring cast. To make matters more interesting, some of the "oldies" were switching to new roles. So there was a lot of learning going on.

This newly assembled combination includes several people with whom I've worked before (always a plus), a few people with whom I felt an easy connection right away, and, even better, a surprising number of Scrabble players. I'd packed my board, hoping to find even one. I easily found four. Then, word spread, and people were reserving spots in the next game. My kind of folks! It's a very nice group. Very social, very inclusive, very accessible. The oldies were extremely supportive of us newies. And everyone seems to have a real love for the show. As I got to know my new family of funny, interesting show people, I sometimes felt vague twinges of guilt, as if I were cheating on my *Producers* family. But that's the nature of the profession. You form fairly close relationships fairly quickly, and then part ways. Constantly. And then one morning I was walking by a shop window, and there they were: my former cast mates, smiling up at me from a poster advertising their upcoming engagement at the Fox. And I somehow felt absolved.

One of my favorite new experiences is being in a show with kids—four of them. I quickly bonded with Lois Yaroshefsky, the schoolteacher (a funny, outgoing New Yorker with whom I share in common a love of kids and a background in improv comedy), and with Erika, a terrific, smartass ten-year-old kid and veteran of the previous tour. She and Nadine (a "new-new," like me) alternate in the roles of young Cosette and young Eponine. Daniel and Branden alternate in the role of Gavroche. Branden's older brother Justin played the role previously, until he got too big.

On our first day off, I accepted an invitation to join Lois, Erika, and her grandparents for a trip to a place called Stone Mountain for Erika's birthday. Why not? Nice, solid stone sounded great after all that turning. Stone Mountain is a huge monument. It's like Mount Rushmore in that the main feature is a vast, carved portrait in the side of a rock—this one depicting Jefferson Davis, Robert E. Lee, and, most appropriately, "Stonewall" Jackson. But what makes Stone Mountain kind of goofy is that it was never quite finished. Apparently, the project was plagued by problems. The first designer quit mid-carving, taking his designs with him. In the years that followed, several attempts were made to complete the monument, only to be halted by a lack of funding. Nevertheless, there's enough there to merit the existence of a small theme park, just perfect for a ten-year-old birthday girl dragging along four old adults. (Treat yourself to a chuckle and have a look at *www.stonemountainpark.com*.)

We had a terrific time. We took the skyway to the top of the mountain, then down again, paddled in paddle boats and got sopping wet, visited "Stoney, the Talking Fountain" and got even wetter. To dry off, we watched a glass blower at work and rode a train. Then we went to "The Rain Wizard Show" where, much to our delight, we got sopping wet all over again—perfect for a sultry Atlanta summer day. I felt bad that I didn't have a present for Erika, so when we stopped in Stone Mountain's candle shop (not sure what candles have to do with incomplete mountain carvings, but anyway . . .), I treated us both to do-it-yourself candle dyeing. She daintily dyed her two sunflower candles in carefully chosen complementary shades— instant art. Mine looked like a botched rehabilitation project for the criminally insane. That brat . . . *consoled* me! The nerve of that kid. I think we've bonded.

Back at the theatre, we were moving quickly and smoothly through rehearsals. We learned music, talked character, and rode around and around on the big Lazy Susan stage. One day revolved into the next as, little by little, the show was cobbled together. Each day, I had some new bit of good news: Tuesday, I tried on my costumes, which are brilliantly detailed. I play an innkeeper, so the lace cuffs on my shirt are frayed, singed, and stained with wine. In fact, nearly everything is delightfully dingy and sloppy, and fun to wear. Wednesday, more good news: I've been directed to squeeze the "wenches" in my tavern. Apparently, this is part of my job, and the wenches are expecting it. Amazing. On Thursday, I met with the make-up people, to learn the make-up design for my character, which includes large amounts of "dirt"—sponged-on brown and black pancake that everyone in the show wears. I also get to black out my teeth and go days without shaving. Life is good. My dressing room, I discovered on Friday, was on the same floor as the kids' and their schoolroom. Often, I'd be sitting there and the four little knuckleheads would come visit and make me laugh. With me seated at my make-up mirror, we're all about the same height. They're even funnier up close.

Opening night was there before we knew it. It was a relatively quiet event, celebrated afterwards at the hotel bar. And off we went: the new national touring company of *Les Misérables*. Jason and Dale left, and our Atlanta run, as well as our tour, had begun. Though I play the "Master of the House," I still didn't feel I'd mastered the role, but that was fine. It's good having room (and the director's blessing) to grow in a part. Besides, I'd only had two weeks of rehearsal! So far, it still felt like I was running to catch a moving train, just inches from grabbing the handrail and being on my way. On track, you could say, but not yet on board. Even still, it was joyous. I often stood backstage thinking, "I can't believe I'm in *Les Misérables*." After years of waiting to play this role, it had all happened so fast.

And Atlanta was loving us. The way this show moves people makes me so proud to be a part of it. I'd forgotten how really great it is. Fans return over and over again, bringing their kids and spouses, and wait at the stage door for autographs afterwards. It's uplifting, this show. It *enriches* people. And there's something very—I don't know—"rustic" about the whole thing. It feels like we could be doing Shakespeare in the woods somewhere. The camaraderie, the rags, the jovial, joking nature of the cast, the show's famous barricade set, made of chairs and pieces of wooden railings, the "dirt" we wear, the story of the struggles of the common man—it's all very earthy. Such a contrast from the gorgeous tailored urban glitz of *The Producers*. Two great shows, both highly entertaining, but in vastly different ways.

And while Atlanta was loving us, we were loving Atlanta. Most of us had way too much Southern cooking. Gladys Knight's soul food restaurant was dangerously close. I could have gladly lived on their tasty fried chicken, greens, and grits while listening to their collection of '70s R&B recordings. Then there was Merry Mac's Tea Room. I don't know why they called it that. The tea was iced, and served mainly to wash down the biscuits and gravy. There were many evenings when you could hear moans from the girls' dressing area as they reluctantly cinched up their pre–soul food-sized corsets.

Tonya and I (Tonya plays the role of Fantine) joined the school field trip to the Martin Luther King Center, then to Ebenezer Baptist Church, where Dr. King's father had been pastor, and then to his childhood home. King has always been a hero of mine (as he's been to so many), so the whole day was highly moving for me. There were a few moments when I had to separate from the group and just take it in. And I got to help teach the kids about the importance of his work.

And then, it was time to pack. Here we go again, folks. Off to Dayton, then to Cleveland (ugh . . . why? *Why??*), then Flint, Springfield, West Point, and so on, and so on. How long will this particular adventure last? How many revolutions on this revolving disc? Hard to say. I have a general plan, but we all learned in my last installment how plans can change. We'll see. To quote Atlanta's most famous fictional resident, "Oh, fiddle-dee-dee . . . I'll think about that tomorrow."

Kostroff

14
SON OF CLEVELAND

Jenny Bates is a fun, lively, nerdy-chic young woman who handles our publicity for *Les Misérables*. She's smart, and a real theatre lover, so I liked her right away. And, since I always volunteer for any interviews, post-show talkbacks, lecture opportunities, or school visits that may come along, the woman, naturally, adores me. It's a thing I do. Whenever I start a new show, I go to the people who coordinate such things and let them know I'm available. I really enjoy that stuff, especially talking to students. Maybe I like the attention, or maybe I feel I'm "paying it forward": When I was a young guy, experienced actors were often generous with their knowledge. So I feel that it's part of the tradition. I find it fulfilling, sharing what little I know.

I got a call from Jenny one afternoon while we were still in Atlanta. "So Michael, my friend, I've got *four* telephone interviews lined up for you!" she chirped.

"Great! For what city?" I asked.

"Cleveland."

Cleveland? *Cleveland*?? Oy. My last visit, with *The Producers*, was one of my strangest experiences in recent memory. (See chapter 4, "The Dark Mysteries of Cleveland.") What could they possibly want with me?

Jenny continued: "Oh, and also, the theatre wants to know if you'll teach a master class to some local drama students."

"Cleveland?" I repeated. "Really? A master class? Me?"

"Oh yeah! Apparently you're huge in Cleveland," she joked. "First of all, they're big fans of *The Wire* there, plus, a lot of people saw *The Producers* last year, plus, they love *Les Mis*, and you're Thénardier, for Pete's sake! You know how thrilled they're going to be?"

Okay . . . so, four telephone interviews later, Cleveland was abuzz with talk of my return. Okay, not really. But it was more attention than I'd ever expected from the city I lambasted so ruthlessly last year. Don't these people read *Letters from Backstage?*

Actually, I did look forward to being back at the City Court Apartments there. Something about that weird, semi-seedy building really appealed to me. It's terrifically self-contained (you may recall), with a laundry room, swimming pool, dry cleaner, grocery store, bar, coffee place, and Subway sandwich shop, all in the building. And the apartments are bright and spacious, with lots of closets . . . ugh, I sound like a real estate ad. Anyway, I liked it there, in spite of the vaguely funky smell and general dinginess . . . or maybe because of it.

But Cleveland's City Court and the Michael Kostroff Fan Club would have to wait. First, we were booked for two weeks in another Ohio town, Dayton.

I'm often surprised by the extent to which smaller U.S. cities have been infiltrated by big-city culture. Go to any moderately sized Midwestern town these days and you'll find an "alternative" newspaper, New Age practition-ers, lily-white local boys in hip-hop gear hanging out on street corners doing their best approximation of black gangbanger slang, and restaurants serving trendy, multinational cuisine.

Such was the case with downtown Dayton. I was all set to scoff at the cast mate who requested balsamic vinegar at the Pizzeria Uno. I mean, it's *Dayton*, right? But the waiter didn't bat an eye. "Of course, sir. Regular or tarragon?" Balsamic vinegar, along with things like raspberry iced tea,

Thai chicken sate, cilantro walnut pesto, sun-dried tomato couscous, and Portobello mushroom bruschetta, has become standard—as common in the culinary landscape as salsa. These things aren't even considered exotic anymore.

Downtown areas are often bleak, but Dayton's was nearly a ghost town. Day or night, you rarely had to wait for the light to cross the street, because there was hardly any traffic. It was a little sad. And yet, while most of the city closed early, there were big crowds at the show every night. And in the lobby of the huge, modern theatre, we discovered an eatery that stayed open after the show, serving pan-seared scallops and miso soba noodles, of course. Le Dayton was on the cutting edge of au courant!

Jenny had set up a behind-the-scenes tour for a huge group of high school and junior high school students who were all enrolled in the same theatre training program. It was at the crack of 11 AM or some other shockingly early hour, but stage manager Peter and I roused ourselves and went to the theatre to meet them. There must have been a hundred kids there, and taking all of them through our narrow backstage area was challenging—not unlike squeezing peanut butter through a straw. Nevertheless, it was fun, and they had great questions.

But for me, the highlight of the school tour was meeting a fellow Thénardier! Recently, a special "school edition" of *Les Misérables* was created, and approved for production. So schools all over the country are now doing the show. So, in Dayton, this string bean comes up to me and introduces himself, and tells me that he played Thénardier at his high school. I was so tickled! We shared a few laughs and compared notes.

He turned out to be just one of several young Thénardiers I'd meet in my travels. What I love is that they're always the more interesting, unusual-looking guys—tall and thin, or short and round, with that special spark that funny guys have. We should form a club.

During the Dayton run, I was excused for several shows so I could return to LA to film my third episode of *King of Queens*. They'd booked me before the tour started, and *Les Mis* had agreed to release me. Fortunately, my role was in good hands. My two understudies, Michael St. John and Chip Leonard—both funny, great guys, one tall and thin, one short and round—each got to go on.

It's interesting. Though most people think of television as the more glamorous medium, TV folks seem to be awe of those who do big stage musicals like *Les Mis.* So many TV actors either started off in Broadway musicals, or wanted to. And so the people on the set at *King of Queens* had all kinds of questions. They wanted to know what it was like to be out on the road, performing such a well-loved classic for such huge crowds every night, and I enjoyed sharing with them.

As soon as the shoot was over, I went straight from Sony Studios to LAX, took the red-eye, and landed in Dayton the next day, in time for the Saturday matinee. What a life.

I could tell that Chip and Michael had done well as Thénardier. You can always tell. Here's how: When you return from missing a performance, if your understudy was bad, no one comes right out and tells you. That would be gossipy and ungracious. Instead, they clap you on the shoulder, look meaningfully into your eyes, and say, "*Really* missed you," in a way that lets you know that the show suffered while you were gone. Fortunately, that didn't happen. I got, "Hey! Good to see you!" and, "Welcome back!" but no hidden meanings.

Okay . . . so . . . Cleveland . . .

To refresh your memories, the last time I saw Cleveland, it was grey and bleak, then suddenly cold. My coworkers and I descended into a mysterious funk. Several people got sick. It was ugly and stressful, and we couldn't wait to leave.

Fade out. Fade in. Title: "Approximately One Year Later"

Cleveland is unseasonably warm for October. A perfect 70-ish, in fact. The sun is shining. The citizens are happy and smiling. And it stays like this for the whole week we're there.

I'm in a good place with the show. By now, getting on and off a rotating turntable stage seems so normal to me that I'm not sure I'll ever be able to perform on a stationary platform again.

Meanwhile, I'm experiencing the ease that comes with playing a city I've played before. "Familiarity breeds *content*," you might say. I know where everything is: the Kinko's, the Subway, the pharmacy, the card shop, the laundry room, and so on. In fact, I'm helping others get acclimated.

On a night off, I gathered together a group from the show and introduced them to Fat Fish Blue, a great Cajun restaurant right in the downtown area. Last time through, Greg Reuter, one of the swings on the *Producers* tour, had introduced me to the place. He'd first been there when he was touring in *Fosse*. And so it goes. My Fat Fish virgins flipped for the food, and I expect they'll take a new group of tour pals there the next time *they* play Cleveland.

At the theatre, I'm greeted warmly by several dressers who still remember me going on for the first time as Max Bialystock. My former dresser (the one who wouldn't let go of the pants so I could put them on) is mercifully absent.

I'm particularly dreading that endless hike to and from the male ensemble dressing room, which I still recall all too well from last time, and I'm *really* not looking forward to making that trek in my nineteenth-century heels. But this time, the stage manager has assigned me one of the principal dressing rooms, just one flight up from the stage. What a difference!

And good news continues to accumulate: The daily rate at the City Court Apartments turns out to be seventeen dollars less than what was quoted.

And everyone I meet is friendly and intelligent.

All in all, things couldn't be more different from my last visit. I don't know what to tell you, folks. "Cursed Cleveland" was welcoming me back with open arms. Even the beautiful, warm weather seemed to be saying, "Oh, hey . . . Sorry about last time."

On Thursday at noon, I go to the theatre to meet the local arts education administrator, who leads me downstairs to a small basement theatre space to teach my master class. Most of the attendees are students from a local arts high school. Others are just theatre fans who are interested in what actors have to say about their work. Now, the whole idea of me teaching a master class cracks me up. What exactly it is that I'm supposed to have mastered is beyond me. All those years of barely making a living, when I couldn't get arrested as an actor, nobody knew from me. Then suddenly I book a few jobs and I'm teaching a *master* class—a guy who never even went to college. I give up.

I decided not to plan much, because I always like to see where the group is at and answer as many questions as possible. That way, I'm tailoring my class to the needs of the students. Not planning turned out to be a good plan.

I told them a little about my particular journey, being a late bloomer in the professional world. And I gave my usual shpiel on how hard it is to make a living as an actor. Then I answered a flood of questions, on everything from agents and managers to dealing with upstaging actors to figuring out your market*. They asked about unions, headshots, tour life, and so on. Several of them performed their prepared monologues, and I taught them a few of my favorite acting tricks. We went way over the allotted time, but it was too much fun to stop.

The next day, when I arrived at the theatre, there was a gift waiting for me from the arts education administrator: a thank-you note, attached to a small plastic bag. And inside the bag, Cleveland itself, in chocolate. A chocolate Cleveland! What was next, a key to the city?

Now, Lois, our schoolteacher, who is instant friends with everyone she meets, had struck up a conversation with the owner of a luggage shop

---

*market: In acting, this means the types of roles for which a particular actor is best suited. Knowing one's market is crucial. If Danny DeVito, for example, had insisted on pursuing only tall, sexy leading man roles, he probably wouldn't have had much of a career. Instead, he was smart enough to know the types of characters that suited him, and for that we are forever grateful.

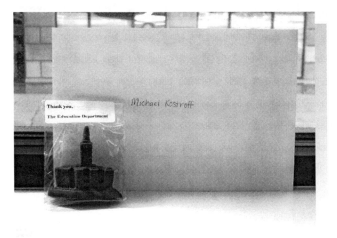

What was next? A key to the city?

near the theatre. "You gotta go meet him!" she urged me. "He and his wife saw you in *The Producers*, and I think they saw you play Max! He really wants to meet you!"

So, on our last day in town, I swung by the store and introduced myself. Great guy. He was surprised to learn that the matinee he and his wife had attended was my Max debut, and I was relieved to hear that they couldn't tell. Standing amidst the suitcases and valises, we chatted about theatre, Cleveland, road life, and so on. And as I walked out of his store into the beautiful, sunny, warm Cleveland autumn day, I thought "*Okay*!!! I *give*!!! Cleveland's not so bad after all!"

Mind you, I wouldn't want to live here, but it just became a nicer place to visit.

Here's hoping you all find the sunnier sides of your own Clevelands. Stay tuned for more adventures.

Kostroff

15
A FLICKER OF FLINT

October 21st, 2003

Greetings, friends. Hope you're all well.

Out here on the road, the days, and the cities, are whizzing by. Since this particular tour consists of mostly one-week engagements, we're packing up and moving nearly every Monday—our day off. Naturally, that can be grueling. But on the up side, you never get tired of any city. Soon enough, the scenery changes.

As for me, I'm finding that the joy of being in this great show—and, in fact, the joy of making a living as a professional actor—more than sustains me . . . at least for now: If there's one thing I've learned about touring, it's that one's attitude can change as swiftly as the scenery. If you've been a follower of *Letters from Backstage* for a while, you've probably noticed that pattern. You may also have observed that on the road, as in life in general, experiences are often a matter of perspective—where you're "at" (mentally), more than where you're *at* (physically). I've learned that over and over. My recent return to Cleveland was a great illustration. Same place, two visits, two different experiences.

And, while I am a staunch *dis*believer when it comes to the idea of "creating" good things through "positive thinking," I nevertheless adhere to a strict policy of being ever-mindful of the strong possibility that I am 100 percent full of shit on any particular subject. I do know this: If you're *able* to look on the bright side, if indeed there even *is* a bright side to your circumstances, then, well . . . it certainly doesn't hurt. It beats the hell out of whining. And so I'm afraid that I've become a reluctant glass-half-fuller.

Flint, Michigan, was immortalized in Michael Moore's brilliant documentary, *Roger & Me*. I highly recommend it if you haven't seen it. Among other things, it presents a city that was once economically healthy, supported mostly by the Ford auto plant where most of the citizens worked. But when Ford closed up shop, abandoning its loyal workers, many were plunged into poverty. It's pretty bleak.

But I never saw that Flint—the one with the closed factories and "Going Out of Business" signs—only the small corner of it where the Holiday Inn Express sits near a curved highway interchange in the middle of nowhere.

I checked into my modest room. Nothing lavish, but perfectly fine for a one-week stay. The late afternoon autumn sun shone through the single window, which looked out on the hotel driveway's overhang. Beyond the parking area, past a few feet of grass, cars whizzed by intermittently. Beyond that, on the other side of the street, in the middle of a large parking lot, I noticed a long, low building, with stalls outside. A farmers' market! These, I thought, are the things that make each place unique. I left my suitcases packed, and headed back out to explore.

Crossing that highway interchange was a perilous adventure in itself. There was no crosswalk or light. You just had to make an educated guess and go for it. But once on the other side, the farmers' market proved nearly worth the risk of being run over. It was warm inside, and there was an eclectic collection of wares from local merchants: In addition to the usual fresh produce, there were used books and CDs, silk flowers, homemade jam, soap, incense, even an art gallery. But first things first: I was hungry. At the far end, I found a vendor whose menu included a fantastic homemade chili. There was a little café upstairs, but it was closed. In fact, opportunities to dine there were elusive. It was only open until 3 PM, and only on the three days a week when the farmers' market was open: Tuesdays, Thursdays, and Saturdays. The word was that the food there was great and homemade, and that there was usually a line to get in. Well, of course there would be, since there wasn't much else in the area. I learned all of this, and other interesting facts, from the woman who sold me the delicious chili. The market used to be open seven days a week, she told me. But, like a lot of things in Flint, it fell upon hard times and nearly shut its doors permanently. It was rescued when the city leased the market to the Uptown Reinvestment Corporation, which now runs it. Happily, business is on the upswing, but only enough to sustain three days a week. I asked if she'd ever seen *Roger & Me.* I had to remind her what it was. "Oh, no. I heard about that movie. Most of us aren't too interested in seeing that." I got the same answer from everyone I asked.

We all spent a fair amount of time at the farmers' market that week. When the café was open, we lined up with the locals to get in. It was like waiting at an exclusive New York dance club, hoping the bouncer would admit you, or like visiting Seinfeld's "Soup Nazi." The day I went to lunch there with Tonya, the man behind us in line meekly asked if he could join us, rather than take a whole table to himself. He wanted to free up the next one for a larger party. It seemed only right, and we lunched with a genuine Flintian, who ended up coming to see the show.

The market itself was a great boon, especially for those in the company who are into health food. They stocked up on nuts, vegetables, fruit (both fresh and dried), homemade vegetable soup, local honey, and so on. It seemed there were about 162 varieties of apples alone, all fresh from the tree. Even the less healthy among us came along, just for the browse. We all learned the market's hours very quickly, and the place was always hopping . . . when it was open.

On the other side of the hotel, just across the parking lot, was the other establishment that experienced a sudden surge in business that week, the

China Sea. It was no more than a slightly-below-mediocre Chinese buffet, with a bar—which was roughly the size of a Volkswagen Bug—in the middle of the room. But with no restaurant in the hotel, and the farmers' market closed more often than not, believe me, readers, the China Sea was The Place to Be. Now, when I say there was nothing else around, I mean that we were practically on an island, a concrete island, amidst a sprawling sea of crisscrossing streets and overpasses. There may have been other places in the vicinity, but I never found them.

It was perfectly all right. If *Les Misérables* had been playing on a desert island that week, instead of a concrete one, we'd have all learned to make fire, catch live fish with our bare hands, and build thatched huts from palm fronds. Instead, we relished our steam table cuisine, embracing it as part of the adventure of touring. We even convinced them to stay open late for post-show drinks. The owner was thrilled. The kitchen was normally closed at that hour, but when he saw the potential for more sales, he started cranking out egg rolls by the panful. And that became our post-show meal. Egg rolls and martinis. One night I even brought my Scrabble board. I don't think the staff knew quite what to make of us, but they were glad for the business.

The granola crowd, of course, avoided the China Sea like the plague. People have various ways of living on the road, and the health-conscious have to be especially creative. Cindy, for example, who plays my wife, travels with her own hot plate, pots, and pans, so she's never stuck eating at the local greasy spoon. Me? I take potluck, and enjoy the experience. "When in Rome," and all that.

Now, you may well wonder: Why Flint? How did this particular town get on the schedule? I can't say I have the answer to that. But to me, there's something poetic about *Les Misérables*—a story in which the poor rise up against an unfeeling establishment—playing a town like Flint, where people have been sold out by big corporations. True, it may be that only the unfeeling establishment can afford tickets, but I like the idea of them seeing this show as well. *Les Misérables* champions the underdog, makes us care about the poor. Not to be grandiose, but it may be a story they need to hear.

On opening night, I put on my coat, grabbed the map provided by our company managers, and headed for the theatre. I walked along the wide street that ran past the China Sea's service entrance. I crossed over a freeway, down a long block, and across the street, onto a campus parking lot. There was no roadside marquee. One of our trucks, parked near the street, was the only sign that our show was playing there. It took some hunting, but I found the stage door, down a steep ramp at the far end of the lot. The backstage space was so limited that our company managers were set up in a trailer office outside.

Yes, things were tight. At our usual first-day-in-a-new-city notes session, our stage manager urged us to stay to the right and keep moving while in the hallways, as they were just barely wide enough for two people. If you stopped to have a conversation, you were in someone's way. There wasn't any place for the kids' schoolroom, so during the show, we'd see them huddled with Lois around a small folding table by the loading dock, trying to play a board game without making any noise. In the doorway at the end of one hallway, our crew had installed a step unit that led directly to the stage floor. Three more feet and you'd be in nineteenth-century France.

I wish all of you could watch a big musical like ours from backstage some day. It's a remarkable thing. But we wouldn't have had room for you in Flint. We barely had room for the ball gowns.

Flint, as you may have figured out on your own, isn't what you'd call an "A city," in the language of those who book touring shows. It's never going to be the first city a show plays. In fact, it's not going to be the second, nor the fifth, nor the twelfth, nor even the twentieth. It's the kind of place you might hit once your show has played all the major and medium-sized cities, as *Les Mis* has. In Boston, Cleveland, San Francisco, Cincinnati, and other major cities, there are people who make their living doing theatre full time. Not so in a city like Flint. And as such, your local crew members may not get a whole lot of practice doing whatever it is they're doing.

One of my cast mates was greeted by his dresser—a little old lady with a very scattered energy—like so: "Hi! I'm so-and-so. I've never done this before. I'm *so nervous!*" And she was. She handled her nervousness with jokes. Jokes in lieu of the much-needed garments my poor cast mate was awaiting during his fast costume changes. But after a few nights, her nervousness gave way to a sort of quiet frozen terror, which is where she plateaued for the remainder of the run.

My dresser was an unusually eager young woman. Whenever I'd approach the dressing area, she'd leap from her chair and assume a wide stance, with her knees slightly bent, her hands spread in front of her, and rock back and forth, prepared to catch, one might assume, a flaming cannonball if necessary. I believe this woman would be ready, willing, and able to administer CPR or deliver a baby at a moment's notice. There was a generalized busyness about her, and her hyper-vigilance made it difficult for her to let me go once I was dressed. She'd follow, yanking on my collar, straightening my rags, pulling on the hem of my smock, right up until I was onstage. My instinctive reaction was to project a dead calm, in the hopes that it would be contagious. So for each costume change, I'd slowly, gingerly approach the dressing area, patting the air in a calming gesture, and say, in the reassuring tone of a hostage negotiator, "Please . . . don't get up. I'm fiiiine. Eeeeverything's cool. We have alllll the time in the world." It takes a certain personality to be a good dresser. She didn't have it. (In her defense, it wasn't her usual gig.)

But all of this merely served as amusement. Nothing upset me in the least. Like I said: perspective. And that week, I was blessed with a good one. I enjoyed the oddity and bittersweet charm of this off-the-beaten-track tour stop. In fact, to me, it was a little bit beautiful. And how often would I be in Flint? And . . . it was only a week, which added a lot to its appeal.

One week more of the China Sea's greasy egg rolls and my one-woman SWAT team, and I might have been screaming a very different tune.

But while we're here, here are a few snapshots:

One night after the show, as we crossed the campus on the way back to the hotel, a few of us paused by a playground area. A row of swings hung there, empty, in the darkness. We all decided to swing a bit before heading home. I can't tell you the last time I was on a swing. We started slowly, but before you knew it, there was that nostalgic squeak and clanking of chains as some of my younger associates started going for it full throttle. Other colleagues, passing by, smiled and shook their heads. Some decided to join us, and we all laughed like kids, with giddy abandon, swinging as high as we dared toward the night sky.

I hung out one afternoon with Ma-Anne, who plays Eponine. I like her. She's an extremely passionate, talented performer, and uniquely individual. I get the sense that her journey, like mine, hasn't always been easy, and that makes me like her even more. We had lunch, then walked along the path behind the farmers' market. There were beautiful fall leaves on the ground, and they crunched as we walked. We stopped to watch a family of ducks paddling along in the stream. And we talked about life, and touring, and her fantastic five-year-old son.

Before leaving on tour, I'd packed a box of winter clothes and left them in my apartment to be shipped later. My friend who's subletting my place in Los Angeles sent them to me here in Flint (oh, the joys of having a wonderful sublettor), and it was like opening a big Christmas present, since I'd forgotten what I'd packed in that box. The timing was perfect, as it was starting to get mighty chilly.

And soon enough, it was time to hit the road again.

And that was *my* Flint. Some fallen leaves, a freshly picked apple, some interesting locals, a weird Chinese place, some oddball dressers, some major swinging, and eight performances for eight appreciative audiences in a town that doesn't get that many shows like *Les Misérables*. When my head's in the right place, these are the things that make road life such a remarkable gift.

It's also a gift when I hear from you all, so drop me a line when you can. Hope you're all spectacular.

Kostroff

16

"OTHER THAN THAT, MRS. LINCOLN, HOW DID YOU LIKE THE PLAY?"

October 28th, 2003

Dear friends,

Springfield, Illinois, is where Abraham Lincoln spent many years of his life. And that's what it's known for. Now, I wasn't much of a student growing up, so most of what I've retained about old Abe comes from the "Great Moments with Mr. Lincoln" attraction at Disneyland, where, every twenty minutes, a motorized puppet delivers highlights of famous speeches. And that isn't really what you'd call a thorough education. As a result, I'm always inclined to picture the great president as stiff, waxy, mechanical, and repetitive, which really isn't fair. So I promised myself I'd do some Lincolny things while in town with *Les Misérables*. I felt obliged to show some respect. After all, the poor man was shot by an actor.

And so, a group of us got uncharacteristically organized one morning and headed out. We had a map of all the Lincoln sites, and a guidebook, supplied by our hotel. It was a perfect fall day. The sun was bright, the air was cool, and vibrantly colored leaves were everywhere—on the trees, on the ground, and drifting through the air. It's one of the great shortcomings of the English language that there's no way to fully convey how beautiful a day like that can be.

Just a few blocks from our hotel was Lincoln's home—the only one he ever owned and the last place he lived before moving to the White House. As we turned the corner, it was as if we'd stepped back in time. The entire neighborhood had been restored to the way it looked when Lincoln and his neighbors lived there. For a block in each direction from the house, the sidewalks were made of wooden planks. The gravel streets were closed to traffic. It was so quiet that you could hear chirping birds and people's footsteps. It was easy to imagine women in bustles, men with walking sticks, and the clip-clop of horse-drawn carriages.

One of the neighboring houses had been converted into a small museum, and we strolled through it while waiting for the guided tour to start. There were all sorts of documents and artifacts from Lincoln's life: newspaper ads for his law practice, models depicting changes to the Lincoln home over the years, family portraits, tools, utensils, and even a leather stovepipe hatbox.

At tour time, we crossed the little street and joined the group that was filing in. The interior of the house was fully restored, and we savored every detail of this glimpse into the household life of a legendary American. In the kitchen, the tour guide showed us how the Lincolns cooked and ate. We saw the bedroom where the Lincoln children slept and the sitting room where guests were received. But what stood out most to me was the tiny writing desk—the actual one where Lincoln sat to write speeches. It was such a humble little piece of furniture, and yet, history was made there.

After the tour, we walked over to see the Old State Capitol building, which is now a museum. The building is staffed by volunteers dressed in period garb, each of them well versed in all things Lincoln. Then we visited Lincoln's law firm, followed by various other Lincoln and/or

Lincoln-related attractions, all within walking distance. And as one Lincoln experience led to another, I began to feel an increasing sense of guilt, because—well, folks . . . okay . . . I'd become bored. Dear merciful Lord in heaven was I bored. It's terrible. I know. Shameful. And I really tried to fight it, but my brain kept fuzzing over as I looked . . . and nodded . . . and sauntered past one historical site after another until finally, boredom won over guilt, and I had to go back to the hotel and take a nap. I was Lincolned out. Awful. I know. And believe me, I felt ashamed. So ashamed, in fact, that it took an hour and a half to sleep it off.

And I thought about all the things we know we *should* care about, but don't. For example, I have a passion for correct use of the English language. I'm no expert, and I do make mistakes, but I aspire to accuracy. I think language is important, and I think everyone should care about it as passionately as I do. But everyone doesn't. In fact, when I discuss my outrage over the deplorable new practice of using quotation marks to emphasize words (absolutely unacceptable), or the fact that the phrase "I could care less" really means the *opposite* of what the speaker is trying to say, I see in friends' eyes that same glazed-over, far-away gaze that *I* got looking at Abe's actual shoelaces. I wanted to be interested, but I wasn't.

So there you have it. I'm a terrible American. But guilt or no guilt, I was done with the Lincoln portion of our visit. In fact, if I heard one more thing about Lincoln, I was going to scream.

I began to forgive John Wilkes Booth.

In fact, knowing what I now know about Lincoln's life, it wouldn't have surprised me one bit if he himself had said something along the lines of, "Boy am I bored! Somebody shoot me, already!"—never guessing that someone would take him literally.

Anyway, the town itself was charming and cheerful. After the Flint experience, the whole cast appreciated and enjoyed Springfield's wider variety of things to see and do. There was a great place called the Feed Store, which was known for its homemade soups—perfect for October. Cast members were there nearly every day, fortifying ourselves with one of their fantastic concoctions du jour. There was also a Frank Lloyd Wright house, and a funky used book shop, where, while browsing carelessly one day, my eye fell on a tattered little brown pamphlet which, for $2.99, I couldn't resist acquiring. The cover read as follows:

WORRY AND ALLIED FAULTY MENTAL HABITS

BY

G. L. WALTON, M.D.

INSTRUCTOR IN NEUROLOGY, HARVARD UNIVERSITY;
PHYSICIAN TO DEPARTMENT FOR DISEASES OF THE NERVOUS SYSTEM,
MASSACHUSETTS GENERAL HOSPITAL

Read before the Students of the Boston School of Gymnastics
March 6, 1903

PUBLISHED BY
THE BOSTON NORMAL SCHOOL OF GYMNASTICS
97 HUNTINGTON AVE., BOSTON

The cover alone seemed to raise more questions than it answered. Are gymnasts more prone to worry than others? And, is there an *Ab*normal School of Gymnastics? That would be enough to worry anyone. Being, by nature, a worrier myself, I was interested to read what Dr. Walton had to say. Maybe it would help.

Meanwhile, back at the show, I was making an interesting discovery: While technically I was doing fine, I was, by my own standards, not quite "nailing" the role of Thénardier. It wasn't that I was bad in the part–just not knocking it out of the park.

Now, this may sound strange to some of you, but it's my belief that discovering you haven't yet reached your potential is not necessarily such a bad thing. In fact, sometimes, it's excellent. Approached positively, the feeling that you still have quite a bit of work to do can keep you on your creative toes, which means the job can never be dull. And one of the great things about theatre is that tomorrow, you get another chance to be better. And so I resolved to experiment a bit each night–to look for moments I could improve, to try to inhabit the character more deeply, to rethink choices I'd made early on. After all, I'd only had two weeks of rehearsals before being launched on this adventure. Now, with a few cities under my belt, I found myself in an excellent position to regroup and take another look at my approach to Monsieur T. Actually, it was kind of exciting.

Okay, having said that, I must confess–just between us that I was somewhat influenced in my assessment by comments on the message boards at *LesMis.com*, the Web site where fans of the show–"Mizzies," we call them–gather. These hard-core enthusiasts didn't care for me one bit in the role, and had no hesitation about saying so consistently in their post-ings. And I started to think, "How can I give these folks what they want? What have I missed?"

Now, granted, the Mizzies' evaluations aren't necessarily the most expert. Most of them are either teenage girls who have crushes on our younger male cast members and probably dot their i's with little hearts, or people who've seen the show way too many times–in some cases, fifty, sixty, or a hundred–and may have become too personally involved. I'm sorry. That's a lot of times. No one needs to see *Les Misérables* that many times. Shit. Even Victor Hugo wouldn't have seen *Les Misérables* that many times.

I've never quite understood this level of fandom. I mean, by way of comparison, I've been a fan of The Manhattan Transfer for almost thirty years. I've seen them live several times–not fifty or a hundred. Maybe five or six times. I bought all their albums (Yes, albums. Yes, I am old.), then, over the years, replaced them with cassettes, then finally, CDs. I know the names of the group's members, the parts they sing, and many of their songs. Never once have I *dressed up* as one of them to attend a Manhattan Transfer fan party. I've never engaged them in imaginary conversations, planned on marrying one of them, or gone into debt to purchase a souvenir. Hell, I just like their music.

Mizzies, on the other hand—well, some of them—take part in an online activity they call "FRP." That stands for "Fantasy Role Play." But you're supposed to know that, or you're not a true Mizzie. These are chat rooms where these folks converse as characters from the musical. As you can imagine, the competition to be "Eponine" or "Cosette" is bloody and vicious, and I'm quite sure that actual crimes have been committed in the obsessive, desperate grapple to lay claim to these coveted positions in the FRP room. I *think* it's a "room." I'm not sure how these things work. I've never visited one of these FRP places, because frankly, I'm very, very frightened of them.

And Mizzies know absolutely everything about the show, even things that people *in* the show don't know. So they'll post remarks on the *Les Mis* message board like:

> "Interesting . . . Julie's dress looked sort of light green during IDAD [That's Mizzie shorthand for "I Dreamed a Dream," a song from the show. You're supposed to know that. And you call yourself a Mizzie.], yet in the Montreal production it was pale blue. They must be ordering the fabric from that new wardrobe shop in Topeka. It was hilarious."

That's the other thing. Everything's "hilarious."

> "Joe's cravat was crooked on the barricade, and his face was like 'uh-oh.' We died. It was hilarious!"

Truth be told, I probably shouldn't have been looking at the Web site, but what can you do? Call it morbid curiosity. Besides, these were members of our public, and I thought there might be something to learn from their comments on my performance.

Not that I was worried about my work. Not *worried*, mind you. Certainly not. After all, as Dr. Walton says on page 12,

> *Try not to worry about whether you will succeed: It only prevents you from succeeding. Put all your efforts into the task itself, and remember that even failure under these circumstances may be better than success at the expense of a prolonged nervous agitation.*

Indeed. And so, with my sleeves rolled up, I was ready to dig in afresh as we packed up and moved the show to West Point, New York.

Life on the road is nice these days. Short stays in interesting places. Fun with the cast. A great role, and room to grow. And, what's even better . . .

As far as I know, no U.S. presidents were born in West Point.

Kostroff

17
MY BROADWAY ADVENTURE

November 2nd, 2003

Friends,

As we move our show from city to city, I find that more and more, I'm choosing to forego air travel in favor of driving with cast mates. There's something great about throwing the luggage in the car, leaving whenever you want, taking your time, and watching the scenery go by. It gives you more of a sense of getting from here to there. Sure, flying is quicker, but doing it every week wears thin. All those airports, with their crowds, noise, bad art, fake air, high security, harried airline workers, and of course, fluorescent lights (you know how I hate those). Compared with that mechanical, glass-and-steel atmosphere, a trip down a highway is like getting back to nature.

And so, instead of flying from Springfield to West Point, I shared the fifteen-hour drive with my very talented cast mate Shahara Ray (she's the Head Whore in the show, and proud of it). Shahara and I had worked together years ago at the Lawrence Welk Dinner Theatre in Escondido, California. (Believe me, I could do a whole chapter on the Welk, with its champagne glass fountain in the lobby and the fake bandstand where you can have your photo taken next to a cutout of Lawrence Welk. But so as not to get too sidetracked, I'll just give you this quick glimpse: The theatre is part of a retirement village. Before the show, the ancient residents are fed a nice meal. Then, they're bused down the hill to the theatre, where they settle into their soft, comfy seats. The lights go out, the overture begins, the curtain goes up, and—you guessed it—everyone goes to sleep. The guys in the pit used to hold up signs for our benefit that read, "SING AND DANCE . . . AND HURRY!" Performers who have trod the boards at the Welk share a special bond. It's an experience.) Anyway, *Les Mis* was a surprise reunion for us.

So off we motored in Shahara's bright orange SUV, stopping at some truly weird truck stops, an enormous video arcade, and most of the Cracker Barrel restaurants along the way.

It was during one of these stops that my agent, Eric, called me on my cell phone. Some of you may remember Eric. You may also remember that whenever he says, "Now here's something interesting," a new twist is about to follow. Last time I heard that phrase, he was about to tell me I'd been offered *Les Misérables*.

"Now here's something interesting . . . First of all, where are you?"

"Hell, I don't know. A gas station somewhere between Springfield, Illinois, and West Point, New York. I could find out the exact town if it's important. Why?"

"They want to see you this week for *Hairspray*, for the Harvey Fierstein role. Can you make it?"

I laughed.

"The drag role?"

"Well, yes. Apparently, they've heard about your legs."

"Well, sure . . . I guess I can get there. How did this happen?"

"Darling, you have me as your agent. That's how."

Well, why not? I hadn't planned on visiting Manhattan, but who am I to say no when Broadway calls?

It was Monday. The audition was on Friday. There were details to coordinate, and not a moment to lose. I swung into action. First question: what to sing to audition for the role of an overworked, overweight Baltimore housewife and mother who turns into a stylish, sassy diva. There is an art to selecting the perfect audition piece, and clever choices are often highly guarded secrets among musical theatre actors. Shahara and I brainstormed as we whizzed down the nondescript freeway. I called my pal Patrick back in LA for his input as well. Patrick has a knack for such things. We all finally hit upon the perfect choice: a song from *Pippin* entitled "Kind of Woman." (*"I'm your average, ordinary kind of woman . . . practical as salt/modest to a fault/conservative with a budget/liberal with a meal/just your average ideal."*) "Stop looking," said Patrick. "That's the one."

The next call was to my sublettor in LA, who found the song in my files (don't ask—I have sheet music for all occasions), and faxed it to our next theatre while agent Eric faxed the scenes I needed to learn. Other details would have to wait until I got to West Point. Everything was in motion—words and images, flying through the air. And it all happened as we zipped along. The wonders of modern technology.

These drives are always longer than you think they're going to be. Especially if you stop at a huge video arcade to kill some aliens. (Well, they had to be killed. The entire universe was in danger, and we were the only ones who could save it.) And so, long after nightfall, we were still traveling. By now, the highway was covered with a thin layer of danger-ous "black ice," and from time to time we'd see vehicles off to the side of the road, some of them overturned. I fought hard against sleep as we con-tinued at a painstakingly cautious speed, our eyes glued to the road. As copilot, it was my job to alert Shahara whenever I spotted a shiny patch, so she could slow down even more. Bridges were the iciest; we crept across them at a snail's pace. Then, some time after midnight, it happened. The SUV hit a slick and started skating around. "Okay . . . okay . . . okay . . . okay . . . here we go . . . okay," I chanted, holding on tightly while Shahara, suddenly very calm, deftly executed a textbook-perfect response, turning into the curve and tapping the brakes, until we spun to a stop against the center divider.

The road was dark. Everything was covered in snow. We were still upright. We were fine. We both exhaled hard; then Shahara turned back onto the road, and off we went. Neither of us was the least bit sleepy after that.

We pulled into West Point at 3 AM, bleary-eyed, shot, and no longer making any sense. I believe we were able to mutter our names to the front-desk clerk, though the process of checking in seemed confusing and foreign at the time. The hotel, a rambling intersection of hallways, built on an incline, was among the ugliest I'd seen in my entire tour of The Great and Not-So-Great Hotels of America. Didn't matter. Not at 3 AM. And not a week away from Boston. We were in terrific spirits, and looking forward to five weeks in Beantown.

And meanwhile, here we were in beautiful West Point, where the fall leaves were even more outrageous than they'd been in Springfield. Here, they were not only amber and tan and tangerine, but also fuchsia and aubergine and flaming orange and flamingo-pink and deep brown, all mixed in together. Our odd hotel had, among its good points, a Denny's and a weird-but-great Greek diner across the street—hallelujah. We were bused daily to the theatre, which was on the campus of the The United States Military Academy at West Point. All in all, not too shabby.

Our company managers had warned us to plan for major, intense, time-consuming security inspections, so on opening night, we left the hotel early enough to allow for lengthy delays at the gate. We pulled up to the guard shack, our IDs out, curious to see what this inspection process would be like, bracing ourselves to make the best of it. This kid with a rifle steps onto the bus and asks, "You guys the actors?"

"Yes."

"Okay. Have a great show." And with that, he steps off, and waves us through. We felt so violated.

Every city's audience has its own personality. The cadet-heavy crowd in West Point was . . . well, not our liveliest. That's because cadets are trained to do things as a unit, in a focused, disciplined manner.

Spontaneous, wildly hysterical expressions of emotion aren't really part of the whole cadet . . . thing. And so, as an audience, they subconsciously organized themselves. All applause was in unison. It lasted for a suitable duration, then ended abruptly. If one stopped, they all stopped. When there was a humorous moment onstage, they responded with no more and no less than the appropriate amount of laughter: a chuckle, immediately followed by silence, so that the presentation could continue.

To make matters worse, the seats in the theatre were grey . . . and so were the cadets' uniforms. So, in the half darkness, not only did the house *sound* nearly empty, it *looked* that way too! And so went our opening night.

Between scenes, I continued to plan my Manhattan detour. I decided to be smart and ask for Thursday night off so I'd be settled and rested for my Friday audition. The stage manager granted my request. I'd e-mailed my friends Jeff and Chris (with whom I'd stayed during rehearsals for *The Producers*), who once again offered shelter to their friend, the wayward actor. Since much of the cast lives in Manhattan, and since it was only a forty-minute drive, lots of people were commuting, and I easily arranged a ride. I'd leave Wednesday night after the show, spend all of Thursday in the city, audition Friday, ride back up with my fellow actors, and do the show on Friday night. Music. Lodging. Transportation. Schedule. All coordinated as the turntable revolved and the French citizens revolted.

Before I knew it, the show was over, and it was time to accept our audience's measured, restrained applause. Backstage, we have a blue cue light that signals the cast to return for a second curtain call. Up until West Point, we'd been cued back out at every single performance. But here, for the first time, the blue light stayed off. That's because the applause had ended. The cadets had expressed their gratitude for what seemed an appropriate duration (perhaps there's a chapter on the subject somewhere in one of their training manuals), then stopped. Clipped and clean and never lavish. Eyes front, soldier. You're in the army now.

I was reminded of a story my friend Joy Todd tells about a bawdy, ballsy stand-up comedienne she used to know, who lived next door to a very mousy little old lady. "Oh, I'd just love to come see you perform sometime," said the sweet old thing.

"Honey, are you sure?" said the comedienne. "My act's a little racy."

"Oh, I don't mind."

Well, the night came, and after the show they met backstage. "Well?" said the comedienne, fearing she'd shocked her elderly neighbor. "What did you think? Did you like it?"

"*Like* it? My dear! It was all I could do to keep from laughing!"

Wednesday night, I arrived at the theatre with all my clothing and music for the big day. We left right after the show, and about an hour after the curtain came down in West Point, I was walking into Jeff and Chris' apartment in Manhattan.

They were waiting up, of course, hungry for all the tour dish. It was a lot like those early weeks of rehearsals for *The Producers*, when I'd stumble home after dancing for eight hours and recount the highlights of the day, acting everything out in their living room. How things have changed since then! I'm now on my *second* big show, breezing into town—*by request*, like a Broadway hotshot—to audition for my third. Who am I all of a sudden?

Thursday, after the guys went to work, I rehearsed my song, worked on my audition materials, and walked around my beloved hometown. I had exciting plans that night. In the midst of all my other preparations, I'd arranged a ticket to see my wonderful friend Stephanie Block, who plays Liza Minnelli opposite Hugh Jackman in *The Boy from Oz.* I'm so very proud of her, and I couldn't wait to see her in her first Broadway show.

Meanwhile, my former *Producers* cast mate, Fred Applegate, was currently starring in the Broadway company of *that* show. Fred and I had been the two Max understudies on the road, so there was a bond. I surprised him with a call and we made plans to meet for dinner.

Hours later, we sat at Barrymore's, the legendary Broadway hangout, catching up. "Fred," I said when we'd finished eating, "I want to see that marquee with your name above the title." So we strolled over to the St. James Theatre, and as we turned the corner, I stopped. My jaw dropped open. It really was a fantastic thing to see my theatre pal's name up in lights—every actor's dream! "Oh, Fred," I gushed. "That's amazing."

And Fred, who is by nature solid, stoic, and underplayed—Fred, who barely bats an eye at even the most shocking news—turned a merry shade of pink . . . and *giggled*! "I have to say," he confessed sheepishly, "it's pretty cool."

We headed backstage, where I saw several former cast mates. Laughs and hugs all around. Moments later, I was lounging in the star dressing room (who am I all of a sudden, with the friends on Broadway?), when who should walk in but Stadlen himself—our former Max—for a surprise visit. All three Maxes in the same room! They teased me for leaving *The Producers*, and I teased them about having to work so much harder than I do. And we laughed and reminisced. And then it was 7:30—time to go see Stephanie in her Broadway debut!

I left the St. James and dashed over to the Imperial. Moments later, I sat shifting in my seat as I waited for the show to start. Like a proud parent, I told all my neighbors that my friend was playing Liza Minnelli, and they got excited too. New York theatregoers are the best. They like to share the experience with each other. Later, during the show, the woman next to me gave a nudge and a wink, as if to say, "Hey, she's good!"

And she was. Fantastic. Stephanie is always great. But this was far above and way beyond. To see her, in her red, sequined minidress, surrounded by dancing boys, wowing a Broadway audience, was really something! I recalled that when we worked together, our pre-show mantra was "Kill the people. Kill 'em dead." Well, she killed 'em—stone-cold dead. Blood in the aisles. Not a soul breathing. When I went backstage after the show, I was without words for a minute. (Yeah, I know. Me. Can you imagine?) So we just stood there grinning at each other and laughing. It's quite something to see your colleagues starring on Broadway.

After I left Stephanie, I headed back over to have post-show drinks with my *Producers* pals. As I waited outside their stage door, out from the theatre swept none other than Mel Brooks and Anne Bancroft. I waved sheepishly, not knowing if they'd remember me. "*Kostroff*!" Mel demanded as he grabbed my arm and slapped my cheek. "We gotta get you back in the show! We miss you in the show!"

"Well, Mel, just offer me the lead" is . . . what I wish I'd said. I believe what I *actually* said was, "I we well I just . . . thanks, because . . . I'm sure I'll . . ." or something of an equally eloquent nature.

The ever-elegant Ms. Bancroft smiled warmly (and with perhaps a touch of pity at my incoherent babbling) as they climbed into their limo. And they were gone, leaving me standing there, stunned, beneath the blinking marquee lights. Do I *know* Mel Brooks? Geez! Look at me. Mr. Broadway!

Friday morning, I stopped by Harlequin Studios to warm up before my audition. Harlequin is a deliciously run-down, dingy brown suite of rehearsal rooms in the heart of the Broadway district. It's up a narrow set of sagging stairs, right next door to a gay porn theatre. Take the wrong flight of stairs, and you're in for a very different experience. The linoleum tiles, those that remain, were probably installed in 1960, and approximate a harlequin pattern. There are signed 8 × 10 glossies of long-dead stars on the walls, a candy machine which hasn't worked since the seventies, and the ever-present aroma of cigarettes and coffee. In short, it's seedy vintage New York theatre heaven. I'd warmed up at Harlequin before each of my three auditions for *The Producers*. They know me there. Larry, behind the desk, gave a smile and a wave.

"Hey! *Producers*, right? What ever happened with that?"

"I got it!"

"Good for you! You want room 2B again?"

"Sure. It's my good luck charm!"

2B is disgusting. I love every ugly inch of it.

I didn't have to work very hard at warming up for this one. The role was written for Harvey Fierstein, he of the gravel-voiced basso, so everything is very low. In fact, I had to "warm down."

And then it was time. I walked over to the audition studio and got settled. As I waited to go into the room, I began to reminisce . . .

I had my first real Broadway audition–to be a possible replacement for the role of Epstein in Neil Simon's *Biloxi Blues*–when I was twenty-three years old. I'd been to open calls before, where I'd waited in line for hours with the hundreds of other hopefuls just to sing a few bars of music for an assistant casting assistant, but this was a real appointment, at the actual theatre, for the director himself.

I got that appointment using good old-fashioned Broadway moxie. At a friend's insistence, I'd summoned all my young courage, knocked at the stage door, and handed my picture/resume to the doorman, saying, "The casting director is expecting this." A few days later, to my stunned amazement, they phoned and scheduled me to come in and read.

And so I found myself backstage, at the very theatre where I'd seen the play only the night before (for research), gawking at the set I'd seen from my mezzanine seat, blind with nerves, completely intimidated, wondering how anyone ever manages to do a decent job at these things. I paced. I smoked. I ran over the big speech in my head. And then they called my name, like it was my turn to be executed. I walked out onto that huge expanse of a Broadway stage, shaking script pages in hand. I was a mess. The stage lights were in my eyes, but from the vast darkness of the house, I heard a warm, disarmingly friendly male voice:

"Hi, Michael. Are you all set?"

"Y-yes!"

"Any questions about the material?"

"No!"

"Okay, then. Let's start with the second scene."

"O-okay."

I turned to begin the scene. The voice interrupted one last time.

"Michael?"

"Yes?"

". . . Breathe."

I hope one day to know who that man was, because I'd like to thank him. That reminder has stayed with me throughout my auditioning career. Since then, fortunately, I've gotten much better at the whole process.

"Michael?"

"Yes?"

I stirred from my reverie. *Hairspray*'s casting director was calling my name.

"We're ready for you."

It was my turn. I went in, all smiles and barely nervous (it's always easier when you have a job already), and met the people for whom I'd be auditioning. We had a great time! I did my best to put *them* at ease, which I've learned is crucial: Take care of them. Don't make them take care of you. They had me sing several songs and read several scenes, which is always a good sign, and I made them laugh a lot, which I love. I even remembered to breathe.

It's always great to see how far you've come.

So that was my jam-packed Broadway adventure–kind of like a mini show biz fairy tale. I headed back to *Les Misérables* happy as a clam. In just a few days, we'd be making our way to Boston. We could hardly wait. Meanwhile, there were cadets to entertain, and I felt newly inspired to make those motherfuckers clap long enough to give us that damned blue light.

All the best from the road,
Kostroff

18
WILLIAM DAWES SLEPT HERE

Whether I shall turn out to be the hero of my own life, or
whether that station will be held by anybody else, these pages
must show.
—Charles Dickens, *David Copperfield*

December 10th, 2003

For the second time since going on the road, I'm in love. And for the second time, the object of my affection is a city. The first city I fell for was San Francisco (and who could blame me?). This time, it's Boston. I hardly know where to begin trying to explain what it is that makes Boston so "wicked awesome," as the locals would say, but trust me, it's wicked awesome. It's like New York in that it's an old city, and the locals tend to be direct and straightforward, but it has less hustle and a lot less bustle. It's urban-sharp-meets-Midwestern-solid. And unlike in New York, you don't have to muscle your way through the day.

Everywhere you look, there's some brilliantly ancient building, with a plaque identifying it as the site of Ben Franklin's former dry cleaner, or the first shoelace manufacturer in America, or the first brick, ever.

And whatever *isn't* old is made to *look* old. The local 7–11, subtly imbedded in a vintage stone building, was identified by one of those old-fashioned hanging metal signs over the door, which creaked as it swung in the breeze. I half expected it to read "YE OLDE SEVENE-ELEVENE." The Kinko's and Supercuts were similarly disguised in Early American quaint. Electric street lamps were programmed to pulsate, simulating the flames of old gas lamps. I wanted to dip my quill and write something on parchment, then ring a big bell and read it in the town square.

Knowing that we'd be here for a substantial amount of time—five weeks—and because I am, by now, a terribly sophisticated itinerant stage actor, I had the dazzlingly savvy idea of renting an apartment and taking up residence, like a proper Bostonian. And so I found, through an agency, a fantastic, tiny one-bedroom located on Champney Place, a cobblestoned alley near the top of Beacon Hill. It was less expensive than a hotel, and a lot homier. It even had a fireplace. And everyone in the company, including me, was terribly impressed by my wicked awesome housing coup.

Throughout the following weeks, I had the best of both worlds. I was at once a tourist and a local—soaking in the history during the day, then stopping to pick up food and firewood at my neighborhood market before heading home, fixing an early dinner, and settling in for a late afternoon nap by the fire before going to work. Some days, I'd just strike out, with nowhere to go, and wander. Every time, I'd end up someplace stimulating. It's that kind of town.

Boston in November. Could anything be better? How come no one's written a song about it? The rain-streaked brownstones, the golden leaves, bundled-up college kids, the clip-clop of horse-drawn carriages hauling tourists through the winding streets. It's picturesque, to be sure. But they're never pushy about it. None of San Francisco's Market Street hawkers or Times Square's tourist traps. No LA "Maps to the Stars Homes." Boston says, "Look, we've been doing the whole 'city' thing for a while now, okay? We invented the *toothpick*, for cryin' out loud. [Yes, they really did.] So look around if you like, and let us know if you have any questions. Nothing to get all hyper about."

Whenever the actors arrive at a new tour stop, one of our first tasks is to find our way to the new theatre, and then find our way around backstage.

Help is provided. Our company managers always furnish us with maps of the city, which feature directions to the stage door. Once inside, we follow the trail created by our stage managers: Photocopies of the famous *Les Mis* logo (little Cosette before a tattered French flag), with the caption, "COSETTE SAYS THIS WAY!", are taped to the walls throughout the backstage area. Each one has a destination, like "ORCHESTRA PIT" or "WOMEN'S ENSEMBLE" or "TRAP DOOR," with a hand-drawn arrow. The constantly changing layout of our work area makes these directions a necessity.

And so, on opening night, I bundled up, locked my front door, and went off in search of what would turn out to be my favorite theatre ever: the Colonial.

Across Boston Common, across Boylston Street, around a corner, and down a brick alley, I found a picture-perfect rusty metal stage door. Past the classic doorman's desk stretched long hallways with dark wood wainscoting. Following Cosette's paper arrows, I climbed four flights of stairs, turned down a narrow hallway, and stopped at the weathered wooden door with my name on it. Inside was a small, square room with faded carpet, an old mirror framed by a few light bulbs, a once-overstuffed chair (most likely a remnant from the set of some play), and a tiny, rusty sink in the corner. As a kid, when I fantasized about living the spectacular life of a touring stage actor, this was exactly the kind of place I'd always pictured: beautifully decayed, dripping with history, reeking of old show business, grand in its way. I could imagine the nineteenth-century version of our company, arriving with trunks and carpet bags, everyone in hats, a yapping dog under the leading lady's arm, the men with walking sticks, as we got off our train, rode to the theatre in horse-drawn carriages, and took up temporary residence there, at the Colonial.

By the way, that name-on-the-door thing? *Still* cool. "Neat!" I always think to myself. "I must be in the show!"

The historical Colonial Theatre (everything's historical in Ye Olde Boston) sits wedged into the middle of Boylston Street. It was built in the year 1900, and christened with a production of *Ben Hur* that featured a cast of three hundred and fifty and an onstate chariot race with twelve live horses. You know. Intimate, low-budget kind of thing. Throughout its history, the Colonial has presented the world premieres and out-of-town tryouts of such legendary shows as *Porgy and Bess, Carousel,* and *Annie Get Your Gun.* In the lobby sits a big marble table where Rodgers and Hammerstein wrote parts of *Oklahoma,* and where Bob Fosse once jumped up to demonstrate a dance step. There's still a nick in the table's surface from

Bob's boot. And here's me, performing there. What an honor! I mean, think of it: Merman played the Colonial!

After our usual sound check, we had our usual "actor/dresser bonding." I liked my dresser, Maureen, right away. A salt-of-the-earth, meat-and-potatoes mother of six (she and her husband had three kids of their own, and liked parenthood so much that they decided to adopt three more), Maureen seemed to perfectly embody the Boston character: a tough, unflappable exterior, and a kind, warm heart.

Performing on the stage of the Colonial made me feel like I was on Broadway. It wasn't only the dazzling beauty of this ornate old jewel box, but also the remarkable intimacy of the auditorium. When the music started and the lights came up and we walked out onto the stage for the first time, it felt like the audience was in our laps! Something about the layout of the room connected us with them in a way I hadn't experienced elsewhere. We could see faces. We could hear sighs, gasps, chuckles. When I performed "Master of the House," I felt like the whole theatre was my inn, and every audience member a guest (and potential mark). We were all closely gathered in the same room, breathing the same air, communicating almost as clearly as if in conversation.

Near the end of Act Two, there was some backstage confusion about the placement of one of my costumes, and I couldn't find it. I've handled things better. I got pissy and nervous and anxious. And while I was busy doing all that, Maureen quietly and calmly found the costume, brought it to where I was having my little baby fit, gently touched my arm, gave me a warm smile (you know, like you would with a crazy person), and said, simply, "Here we go. Let's get you dressed." I didn't just have a dresser. I had a temporary mom.

From that moment on, Maureen and I got along famously. She was funny! And I loved listening to her talk with the other dressers. They were all Bostonians, and the accents were as thick as clam chowdah.

"Hey, Mah-reen, did yah daughdah like her paahdy?"

Ah, that accent. I love it. Very hard to pin down: Just when you're getting used to "Pahk the cah in Hahvid Yahd," you'll hear:

"The hoat waadah's out, so now I cahn't take a bahth."

Then there's this diphthong they use. I haven't heard it anywhere else: It's kind of an "uh-ah" sound. A New Yorker drinks "cwauw-fee." In Boston, it's "cuh-ah-fee." But here's the trick: They don't use it in every instance. So you drink it in the "maahn-ing."

Authentic Bostonian employs a complex system of variable vowels, and only *they* seem to know the rules. The name "Boston Common" is a real challenge. A native explained that the right pronunciation is—and this is a bit of a tongue-twister—"Buah-stin Cuah-min." And let's not even get into the "Massachusetts Negative-Positive" ("So don't I" means "Boy, do I!"), or "bu-day-diz," which are those brown tubers from which French fries are made.

Fortunately for you, readers, I found a great Web site where you can learn the whole glorious lingo: *www.boston-online.com/glossary.html.* If you're planning a trip, I suggest you start studying now. Believe me, it's quite contagious. Before you know it, you will have adopted the local tongue. One day, I was on the phone with a friend back home. "Where are you right now?" he asked.

"I'm in my apahtment," I said without thinking. "Why do you ahsk?"

Our entire opening week was terrific. Enthusiastic crowds, good performances, fantastic, on-the-ball local crew members. The citizens of my new favorite city *love* the theatre.

The crowds remained enthusiastic, even during the series of shows we've come to refer to as "Disco Misérables"—so named because, without warning, our computerized lighting board went wonky, and started executing random lighting changes that weren't part of the design, often at the least opportune moments in the show. Lighting is an important element in *Les Mis*, because besides showing you where to look, the lights also distract you away from where *not* to look. Often, crew members are actually onstage, in a patch of darkness, moving set pieces, or cast members are buried in the shadows, about to be revealed. That is, we're *usually* buried in the shadows. During the disco period, there was no guarantee.

At the beginning of the show, Jean Valjean is released from prison. Alone onstage, he tastes freedom for the first time in nineteen years. As he starts off in search of work, he sings, *"The day begins and now let's see what this new world can do for me."* It was in this delicate, theatrical moment, right on the words *"the day begins,"* that all the lights blasted up to full one night, prematurely revealing a stage full of farm workers. Boy, when the day begins, it really begins!

This kind of thing continued to happen throughout a week's worth of performances. The technical guys tried everything. Every night before the show, someone would say, "I think we've got it fixed now." And then we'd get a dim, dark, moody wedding scene. Or blinking lights at the convent. Or no light at the inn. "Disco Misérables."

And then, all at once, everything was fine. Back to normal. Each lighting cue happened flawlessly, consistently, every performance. Disco was dead. I was hanging out by the stage door one night before the show with Paul, our head electrician, and we got to talking.

"So Paul, looks like the lights are back to normal, huh?"

"Yeah."

"What was the problem?"

"I don't know. Old board. We have a new one on order."

"Oh."

He took a long drag from his cigarette.

"You know how we fixed it, right?"

"No. How?"

Paul slid the cardboard sleeve off his cup of Dunkin' Donuts coffee and held it up with a rakish grin.

"One of these."

"You're kidding!"

"Nope. Wedged it into the slot beside the computer card."

"How long can we do the show like that?"

"Forever. It's in there pretty good."

A big Broadway tour of an epic musical based on a timeless literary classic . . . held totally at the mercy of a Dunkin' Donuts cardboard cup sleeve.

There was so much to see and enjoy in Boston. And each establishment had a story. Walking home late one night, Lois and I stopped off in a pub for a drink. "You know," the bartender volunteered, "this is the oldest pub in America." When pressed, he admitted that the pub had actually been moved, in its entirety, from its original spot, which was, in fact, the site of the first pub in America. Still, that is one old damned pub!

When my friend Sue came to visit, we tagged along with Lois and the kids on the *Les Mis* school field trip. They'd chosen the Freedom Trail—a ninety-minute guided walking tour of historic Boston sites, sponsored by the Parks Department (now let's remember to practice our accents on that one). Tour guides can be hit-or-miss, but ours was deep, eloquent, passionate, subtle, and engaging. "Imagine what that must have been like," she said as we stood before the Old State House, where the Declaration of Independence was first read aloud, "to hear those beautiful words of freedom for the first time ever. Think how radical they were, and what those first listeners must have felt." Then she was silent for a moment. And

I think we were all surprised to feel our eyes welling up in a surge of unexpected patriotism.

We visited Faneuil Hall, the Old South Meeting House, the Boston Massacre site, and several other locations, all thoroughly interesting. Then, after the tour, we went to the house of Paul Revere, where the kids got to dress up in the clothing of the day.

Did you know that Paul Revere never said, "The British are coming!"? In fact, there are a number of erroneous items in Longfellow's historic poem. For example, Paul didn't work alone. William Dawes, who also took that "Midnight Ride" (via another route) was never even mentioned! That's probably because "Dawes" wasn't as easy to rhyme, while "Revere" is a rhymer's dream: Hear, dear, near, cheer . . . well, you get the idear. Or maybe Paul just had a better publicist. At any rate, I'd like, if I may, to correct this tragic historical oversight right here and now, with a poem of my own composing. A poem I call . . . *The Midnight Ride of William Dawes.*

> *Listen my children, without guffaws,*
> *To the Midnight Ride of William Dawes*
> *He had a horse, and rode it well*
> *That other guy can go to hell*

An upstanding man—that was one of his flaws
He stopped at red lights, not to break any laws
Through streets and through towns, and all for the cause
Rode the brave unsung hero named William Dawes

'Tis a sad, sad tale, that always awes
That Midnight Ride of William Dawes
He yelled, "They're coming!" for all to hear
"We know!" said the townsfolk. "We heard it from Revere!"

He made it to Concord, after many a pause
But the British were waiting for poor William Dawes
They had him arrested, and wrapped him in gauze
He was menaced by lions, who showed him their claws
Hammered with hammers, severed with saws
(None of this happened, but it all rhymes with "Dawes")

Oh, listen my children, and you will hear
Of the guy who rode, like Paul Revere
A patriot, robbed of his rightful applause
That well-meaning horseman, polite William Dawes

Requests for inclusion in poem anthologies should be directed to my agent.

Glad I could clear that up.

Back at the theatre, we were continuing to enjoy some of our best audiences ever. Most nights, when the show was over, we were greeted at the stage door by hardcore Mizzies, some of whom saw the show several times during the run. It's a tricky thing, this actor/fan juxtaposition. After the show, most of us are in a hurry to get ourselves to some food, a bar, or a bed. And yet, the attention is nice, and yet, there's a limit, and yet, we don't want to be ungracious, and yet . . .

It's such a strange dynamic. On the inside, very few of us feel like any-thing more than just normal human beings, with hang-ups and insecurities and problems. Just people going to work and doing our jobs. But some fans seem to feel there's a great chasm between us and them. They approach shyly and cautiously, if at all, and treat us like some sort of superhuman, spectacular creatures. I suppose some performers buy into it, but for most of us, it's uncomfortable in the extreme.

Among the stage door regulars, I began to notice one very enthusiastic fellow who showed up over and over, cornering other cast members in long conversations about their performances. He was an odd creature, this particular man, with a wiry sprig of unkempt hair, a bulbous, constantly runny nose, and a voice that was always just a few decibels too loud. He talked at an unbearably slow cadence. And I inferred from his manner that he might have been mildly mentally retarded. Sweet guy, but I didn't want to get caught in a long conversation with him, so I was glad to remain unrecognized.

One night, I was leaving the theatre. I was famished! All through the show I'd been thinking about the Rock Bottom Brewery's quesadillas and a Margarita. I bundled up and barreled through the stage door, chattering with coworkers, and there he was. "Are you in the 'Master of the House' scene?" he asked, as the others continued on.

"Oh . . . ah . . . No, I'm not . . . sorry."

He looked slightly confused. "Okay," he said. And off I went.

By the time I reached the restaurant, I was already feeling like a bit of a heel. I had my lousy Margarita. But I didn't enjoy it. An hour later, as I walked home across Boston Common, I was thinking about that man, spending his time and money to come to the show over and over again. I saw his face in my mind. And I began to wonder: Where did he live? What was his life like? And how did he afford all those performances of *Les Misérables*? I hated my behavior. Had I really *lied* to avoid talking to him?

I'd become, at least for a moment, one of those horrible performers who treat fans as an inconvenience, dismissing the very people for whom we perform, and who provide our salaries. My God! I'd forgotten about the very people that *Les Misérables* is *about*: those who are sometimes passed over by an unfeeling society.

I woke up the next morning thinking about him. I looked for him that night after the show. He wasn't there.

Days went by. He was nowhere to be seen. I knew I'd get over it, but at the moment, I felt pretty disgusting. Why couldn't I have spared a few minutes to talk to a man who, possibly, hasn't had the easiest life, and who, nonetheless, comes to the theatre, and loves it so much he wants to talk about it? Pretty heartless. Didn't *I* come to the theatre for the same reasons—to find refuge from a difficult life? How the hell did I forget?

This wasn't the kind of man I wanted to be.

So . . . I prayed. I honestly did. I know it sounds dramatic. But I really wanted a "do-over." I believe you get a few of those in a lifetime, and I wanted to cash one in. I wanted another chance to just make myself available to talk with this man, and to give him my full attention. I knew it wasn't going to change his life or anything. (And of course, I had invented everything I knew about him. Maybe his life was just great. Maybe he was a wealthy genius entrepreneur without a care in the world. Who knows?) But I was haunted. I wanted another chance not to lie.

Finally, about a week later, he was once again outside the stage door after the show, and I was so powerfully relieved that I charged right up and introduced myself, shaking his hand heartily. I can't imagine what he must have thought of this sudden enthusiasm, but he was glad to talk to me. I didn't bother to explain the discrepancy about whether I was in the show. We had a good chat, and he told me the parts of my role he liked best, and I told him my favorite parts. He couldn't possibly have known how moved I was.

"Stay right here, John. I have something for you."

"Okay."

I went back inside the stage door, bounded up the stairs to my dressing room, thanking God the whole way, and grabbed the little red book

I'd carried with me throughout the tour: an old copy of the abridged *Les Misérables*. It wasn't much, but it was something.

"Here. I want you to have this. It's just a thank-you for coming to see us so much."

"Okay. Thanks. I already have the book though."

"That's okay. I want you to take it anyway." It meant much more to me than it did to him, and that's fine. But I needed to give him something. Something that was important to me. Something I'd miss. Because John had given me something important. Maybe the most important gift in two years of touring: a reminder of what it's all about. There isn't a Margarita in the world that can give you that.

On our last weekend in Boston came the Great Snow of Two Thousand and Three, making everything clean and white, to match my recovered soul. All told, a near-record 16.9 inches fell—the second-greatest December snowstorm Boston had ever seen. I opened my door Sunday morning to find a wall of the stuff, caked up as high as my waist. The world was bathed in whiteness, with straggling flakes drifting down, gracefully and silently, from out of a pearl-colored sky. I was dazzled. There were dunes, all along the sidewalks, that looked like big scoops of coconut ice cream. (It took me a moment to figure out that there were cars under there.) Hardly anyone was driving, so the streets were filled with incredulous pedestrians, shaking their heads as they looked at each other, smiling, not sure what to make of it all.

Our crew wasn't quite so amused. The coincidence of the Great Snow and the end of our run was bad news for them. The Colonial's back alley is only big enough for one truck (or four horse-drawn carriages and one yapping dog), so loading a show in and out was already a slow process. This was going to make it even slower. These guys really are the unsung heroes of touring theatre.

But Detroit was beckoning, and snow or no snow, it was time to pack it all up again and move on. Somehow, I didn't expect it would be quite so memorable as Boston.

The snow crunched under my sneakers as I slipped and slid my way down Charles Street, dragging my suitcases behind me, on my way to the Colonial for our final two shows. I was thinking how thankful I was that those suitcases had wheels (though at the moment, a toboggan might have been even better), and thankful too that, every once in a while, if you're very fortunate, you get a "do-over."

Cheers . . . or, as they say here, "cheahs." May your holidays be wicked merry and bright.

Kostroff

Boston Common, December, 2003.

19
JIGGERY-POKERY

December 29th, 2003

Hello, readers!

I can still recall back when I was with *The Producers.* I had just been offered *Les Misérables*, and seasoned tour veteran (and fellow cast member) Michael Goddard was going over my itinerary with me:

"Okay, Kostroff. Whadda we got?"

"Well, let's see . . . we open in Atlanta."

"Fabulous. Beautiful theatre. Be sure to eat at Gladys Knight's restaurant."

"Okay. Then Dayton. Then Cleveland, again."

"Eh. What can you do? Go on."

"Springfield, Greenville, Memphis . . ."

"All fantastic."

"Boston . . ."

"Sublime. You'll love it. Great audiences. Then what?"

"Detroit . . ."

And that's when he turned white. He pointed an instructive finger at me and charged:

"Kostroff, do *not* stay downtown. Stay in the suburbs and commute."

"That bad???"

"Kostroff. *Trust* me. Stay out of Detroit."

Indeed, I learned from others that, according to common touring knowledge, Detroit was infamously bleak, not to mention dull, and maybe even dangerous. It's the city no touring actor wanted to see on his itinerary.

And we were headed there for Christmas.

So for the four weeks we played Detroit's Fisher Theatre, I did what most of the cast of *Les Mis* did and signed up for the Marriott Residence Inn in Southfield, about twenty minutes outside of the dreaded metropolis. The company shuttled us back and forth between the hotel and the theatre, and all was well.

I really don't mean to sound like a commercial, but I love the Residence Inns. The buildings are laid out complex-style, and each room is like a studio apartment, with a sofa, two nice big closets, a full kitchen, and sometimes even a fireplace and a small balcony. They set you up with pots and pans and everything. Pretty homey for a hotel room. And since it was now the very dead of winter, and I mean the very *dead*, the fireplace was a godsend. (Oh you bet your ass I scored one.)

And so, happily, I saw very little of you-know-where, with the exception of the day I visited the Motown Historical Museum. That was the one local site I had to visit. I was one of those white kids who grew up on black music, so visiting Motown was like a religious pilgrimage for me. I took the tour, drank in every photo and every caption on every wall, and stood, with great reverence, in the famous Studio A—the very recording studio where many classic soul recordings were made by the likes of the Temptations, Gladys Knight and the Pips, and Stevie Wonder. I was in awe. You can't imagine. I grew up on this music. It was really something to be there where it all happened. And I learned something surprising, and rather moving, about Motown: In a time when it was still rare, Motown was an interracial company. They'd hire anybody who understood the music; they didn't care what color he was. And so, even in the very early days of the civil rights movement, they practiced their own form of anti-segregation, hiring several white employees. And everyone worked successfully, side by side, making that great music together. Beautiful, huh?

Other than that, and the occasional mall trip, most of us were perfectly content to just hunker down at the hotel. And so, miles from the city, and with little to do, the Residence Inn became its own cozy community. We had little dinner parties and Scrabble games, watched DVDs together, shared provisions, hung out, and kept warm, thanks to the good people at the Duraflame log company.

One afternoon, shortly after emerging from my front door, I felt a sudden crush of coldness against the back of my neck. What the hell??? I looked around. Nothing. Then, from behind a bush, I heard the unmistakable cackle of a little girl. Suddenly, another object whizzed past me from another direction, accompanied by a delighted shriek from around the corner of a building. Snowballs! Ohhh, the gauntlet had been thrown down. This was war! I started scooping and packing for all I was worth as the four little *Les Mis* urchins scrambled from their hiding places and ran for their lives, screaming bloody murder. We chased each other all through the complex, hurling our frozen ammunition, laughing, gasping (I more than they) in a spontaneous eruption of late afternoon activity. I'd like to boast to you all of my total and merciless victory over the helpless tots, but the little buggers were quick, and I'm afraid I took more than my share of snowfire. God bless these little guys. They keep us all young.

The Fisher Theatre had been host to *Les Mis* before, and the local crew members loved the show, except for its length. Every night, while Jean Valjean sang the haunting "Bring Him Home"—a second-act classic that never fails to bring tears to audiences' eyes, followed by a long, healthy stretch of applause, this one surly old dresser broad used to cry out as she paced the length of the downstairs dressing area, "Oh Lord, *please* bring his ass home already!"

All in all, it turned out to be a surprisingly nice run.

One Sunday morning, I awoke with a powerful sense of not wanting to go to work. And it seemed foreign to me. I don't usually feel that way. But you know how sometimes when you're not quite awake, you tap into your true feelings, unedited, and, in that semiconscious state, unencumbered by morality or ethics? This was one of those moments.

"Well, Michael," I thought as I returned to my reasonable adult self, "you may not *feel* like going to work today, but it's Sunday, and we have two shows today. And as far as I know, you're in both of them. So you'd better get up and get going. Tough it out. I mean . . . you *have* to go. That's all there is to it.

". . . Right?"

And yet, the powerful urge persisted.

I got up, rubbed my eyes, made my coffee, and assessed the situation. I wasn't sick, so calling out would be unethical. And yet . . . the idea was suddenly so deliciously illicit. Hmm. What to do?

I opened the drapes and took a quick inventory: Outside, it was snowing, windy, grey, and bleak. Inside, it was cozy, warm, and light. I had a fireplace, a full box of Duraflame logs, a television, a sofa, and a cupboard full of food. I thought a bit longer. Snow, wind, cold, wet, two shows . . .

Nope. I'm just not seeing it.

And I did it! Oh readers, I blush to tell you. I indulged. I called out sick. It's so not like me. And I felt wicked and wrong . . . until I hung up the phone. And suddenly, I was sure it was the *only* possible choice for that particular day. It was perfect. I took a "Mental Health Day"—an unofficial term for calling out sick when you're physically fine, but really, truly can't see going to work. (Yeah, like you've never heard of that.) And trust me, a Mental Health Day works like a charm. I stayed in my pajamas, kept the fireplace going all day long, watched TV, took two baths, and cooked delicious food for myself. It was sinfully good. If I remember correctly, I believe there was even an Entenmann's Pecan Danish Ring involved. Well, naturally. Shouldn't there always be an Entenmann's Pecan Danish Ring?

The fact is, as the months and the cities start to rack up, theatre folks do tend to get restless and start bending the rules a bit. And the temptations seem to be even greater in stops like Detroit, where there's a lack of entertainment, and perhaps a dip in the fun factor. (And by temptations, I don't mean the famous Motown singing group, though some say they were greater in Detroit, too.) In fact, the Mental Health Day is among the more innocuous indulgences. Others can be fairly unethical and even downright unprofessional—

And yet here, gentle reader, I feel I must pause . . .

Do I go on, and reveal the awful truths of my profession? Do I burst the bubble for those innocents among you?

After all, full disclosure isn't always best. There are some things it's better not to know, like what exactly is inside those delicious Chinese dumplings we all enjoy so much. Or what therapists *really* think of us. Or whether our president is having highly personal marital problems. Along those lines, I've had quite a heated debate with myself back and forth about this next bit, because it contains scandalous expositions. You see, we stage actors sometimes do things onstage that aren't meant for the audience to see. Silly things. Terrible, shamefully unprofessional things. Things we probably should never tell you about, because they're wrong and awful and terribly, terribly . . . not right.

Nevertheless, damn it, they make for some funny stories. And while I wholeheartedly believe that the actual doing was wrong, I maintain that the telling is not. Besides, it's either that, or I write about all the fun things to do in downtown Detroit, and I'm pretty sure we've already exhausted that topic. And so it is with the utmost hypocrisy that I regale you with the following amusing tales of the onstage shenanigans that happen when (we hope) no one is looking.

Les Mis is a particularly dark show, both thematically and literally. Often, we're upstage, buried in smoke and semi-shadow, and it's there where we get into the most trouble. Those shadows are hotbeds of temptation to fool around and try to make each other laugh.

Early in the show, Jean Valjean, the hero of *Les Mis*, steals some silver from a kindly bishop. But he's caught by the police and hauled back to the bishop's house for questioning. A crowd gathers in the bishop's doorway. They watch in awe as the bishop tells the guards to release Valjean, saying that the silver was a gift. In addition, he gives Valjean a set of silver candlesticks, charging him to use the money to become an honest man.

That crowd formation in the doorway is what we in the show call "the Devil's Playground." The audience is watching Jean Valjean, the bishop, and the guards. Why would they watch us? We're just a crowd. So who'd notice if someone were, for example, to tie two people's costumes together, which happened at least once a week? Or if someone were to casually mention that her water just broke? Or worse.

Shortly before the bishop gives Valjean the candlesticks, one cast member was fond of whispering this ad-lib to the group: "As long as he doesn't give him the candlesticks. I can take anything but that. Please, God—*anything* but the candlesticks." Well, of course, we all knew what was coming. The bishop would hand Valjean the candlesticks and we'd all chuckle as we heard our friend mutter in a faint, shaking voice. "Oh . . . God . . . NO!"

One guy used to always try to sell me his sister. Another liked to lean his full weight on the last person in the clump and try to topple the lot of us. Some would just peer through the crowd at this filthy convict—this dirty-faced animal in rags—shake their heads, and say, "Every night it's the same thing. Some criminal running through the streets with the bishop's silver. That's it. We're moving to another neighborhood."

Most of the cast is in the factory scene—a group of nameless, faceless employees. A fight breaks out, and Jean Valjean himself comes to break it up, admonishing:

"What is this fighting all about? Will someone tear these two apart? This is a factory, not a circus."

Well, one cast member loved turning to whoever was nearby and reacting in shock at this last bit of information, as if she'd been under the false impression that she was indeed working at a circus. "Damn it!" she'd say. "They told me it was a circus. Bastards!"

This evolved. Eventually, two of the men had a nightly bet going, and when the news came out that this was, in fact, a factory and not a circus, one had to hand over his day's wages, furious that he'd once again been duped into believing he'd been working under the ol' big top. Even Jean Valjean got involved. Every once in a while, he'd turn on them and point for emphasis as he sang, *"This is a factory, NOT a circus."*

And then there was Chaînés Night. A chaînés [*sheh-NAY*] is a ballet turn. Hard to describe in print, but it's like stepping quickly and smoothly in a circle with your arms in front of you. It's a common step in ballet. Not quite so common in epic musicals. There are, in fact, no chaînés in the choreography for *Les Mis*. But every once in a while, someone would declare it "Chaînés Night," and performers would look for as many opportunities as possible to insert this absolutely inappropriate and incongruous move into their onstage business, ideally with enough subtlety (or at least speed) that the audience would never spot anything out of place. So, people would chaînés during chase scenes, or while gathering citizens to fight at the barricade, or even, sometimes, if they were very, very creative, during their own deaths. Shameful, yes. Then again, I did warn you.

Now, at first, I was absolutely appalled by the lack of actual *acting* going on in the ensemble of *Les Misérables*. But it was only a matter of time until eventually—I'm ashamed to tell you—I gave way . . .

During a drive between cities, Shahara and I had stopped for a bite at a fast food place. It was the middle of the night, in the middle of who-knows-where, and we were both really punchy from the many hours of driving and giggling and having no idea where we were. As we placed our order, both of us glanced casually at each other, registering the fact that we had both noticed our cashier's eyebrows. They'd been completely plucked clean, and replaced by two perfectly semicircular lines way too high on her forehead to even suggest actual eyebrows. It was like a pair of arches on her head, as if she were subliminally advertising another, better-known fast food chain. As she left to get our food, I turned to Shahara. "Don't look at me," she warned, fighting laughter with all her might.

"But Shahara, I just want to tell you something very important," I said, curving my finger and holding it to my forehead.

"I'm not looking. I hate you," she chuckled. Minutes later, we stumbled out with our food, laughing so hard we had to sit down on the curb.

A few nights later, onstage, in a crowd scene, I caught Shahara's eye and, fixing my gaze on her, I slowly pushed up my knit cap, revealing the two perfect semicircles I had drawn on my forehead in eyebrow pencil. She stared at the floor and whispered, "I hate you, Kostroff," stifling a giggle. I casually replaced my cap and returned to the scene.

In "Master of the House," I greet and serve customers who are visiting my inn. One of my props is a small pad of paper, which hangs around my neck on a long, thin strip of leather. I use it to take orders and write out bills. From time to time, I like surprising my fellow actors with little messages for their amusement.

One night, someone lost her shoe in the factory scene. I don't know how it happened. And I can't fathom why no one picked it up and got it back to her. But there it sat, centerstage, while people walked around it. And then, to get it out of the way, someone had the bright idea to place it on a box, which didn't help at all. It looked like an advertisement for a local shoe store. I'm sure every eye in the theatre was trained on that little lone shoe, wondering where it would end up. Finally, Cinderella found an opportunity to grab the damned thing and put it back on her foot. But by then, I'm sure everyone had noticed.

So when it came time for my tavern scene, I distributed bills to my customers that read, "Our policy: No shoes, no service." They were a step ahead of me. Several of them had already taken off one shoe each and placed them on the table.

Cindy Benson, who plays my wife, had a brief eye irritation, so she was permitted to wear an eye patch onstage for about a week. The first night she performed wearing the patch, my message read, "If anyone has seen my wife's eye, please return it. No questions asked."

But some of the pad pranks took real investment on my part.

At the top of the scene, several customers enter and shout their orders to me. They sing:

"Come on, you old pest."
"Fetch a bottle of your best."
"What's the nectar of the day?"

Well, one night, Gina, who has the first solo, was *slightly* late singing the line. It wasn't the kind of thing anyone in the audience would notice, but we who sing the show every night pick up on anything that's even the tiniest bit different, so we all smirked, teasing her for having to catch up with the music. It's what we do.

"Sorry about that," Gina said later.

"Oh, it's nothing. I hardly noticed," I replied.

During an offstage break, I strolled jauntily into the stage manager's office with mischief on my mind. "Hello there. Have you a copy of the score?" I asked. As luck would have it, they did. "I'll bring this right back." And off I went to the company manager's office, where there's a copy machine. I turned to the page that contained Gina's solo, and made a copy. Then I cut it down to the size of one of my bills, took a highlighter pen, highlighted her lyric, *"Come on, you old pest,"* and taped the page onto my prop pad.

And then I waited. I waited for what felt like an eternity. It was a Sunday night, so I wouldn't have the chance to present it to her onstage until Tuesday. And I couldn't tell anyone, for fear of ruining the gag. It was torture.

Finally, Tuesday came. I waited till my scene, and then, during the first group chorus, I slapped the bill down on the table in front of her. As I danced merrily away, I heard that entire side of the stage scream with laughter behind me, which, fortunately, is absolutely appropriate to the scene.

But I think my favorite of the Thénardier Inn Pad of Paper Pranks was the night we were saying good-bye to Robert Hunt, a talented and very well-liked cast member. After many years with *Les Mis*, he'd decided to leave to star in a production of *Jekyll & Hyde*. We wanted to give him an extra-special Thénardier Inn send-off. So, several of us brainstormed until someone came up with the perfect idea, and we spread the word throughout the cast, so everyone would know what to do when the time came.

Shortly after arriving in the tavern, I presented Robert with a bill. It read:

Tonight's Special: "Dr. Jekyll's Brew"
One sip makes you evil.
One sip makes you good.
Take a look around. We're all drinking it!

Sure enough, cast members had all been instructed to flip back and forth between good and evil every time they took a sip of their drinks. And they really went for it. Without missing a note of the song, they portrayed the most dazzling display of group schizophrenia the stage has ever seen. In fact, the scene was more energized and more focused than I'd seen it in months. It was like an acting class exercise. My tavern was a madhouse that night. As for Robert, he couldn't stop smiling. Later, he said it was the best going-away present he'd ever gotten.

For *her* send-off from the show, Lois, who isn't a member of the cast, was granted a special honor. She got to die on the barricade. It's a *Les Mis* tradition, albeit an unkosher one. They got her a costume and sneaked her into the crowd for the final battle scene, and she joined the revolutionaries in their slow-motion death. Being a ham at heart, she milked it for all it was worth. No one in the audience that night knew they were seeing an extra dying French person, but it was a hoot for those of us in the show.

Now, not all the laughter-inducing moments are deliberately instigated. Sometimes, things just go wrong in funny ways. Mistakes. Slips. They usually happen when we get too comfortable. It never fails. Just when a performer feels he's got the show down and knows what he's doing, he makes the mistake of relaxing. And that's when he's most vulnerable to the theatre goblins that bewitch his tongue, addle his brain, and mock his confidence.

I remember one night in *The Producers*, I ran backstage during "Springtime for Hitler," just as I did every night, for one of my four quick costume changes within the number. My dresser was looking at me strangely. "What?" I asked hurriedly.

"Are you usually here this early?" he asked.

I was annoyed by the stupidity of his question. "Yes, this is when I—" and that's when I heard someone onstage singing what was supposed to be my solo line. And there I was, backstage, dressed as a tap-dancing Winston Churchill, when I was supposed to be *on*stage, dressed as a Nazi storm trooper. I was furious with myself for about thirty seconds, and then I had to laugh and let it go. Nothing I could do about it at that point. After months and months on the road and hundreds of performances of the same show, during which the whole thing consistently ran like clockwork, my brain had decided, just this once, to make an unscheduled left turn, smack-dab into a wall.

Reliably, not only did my cast cover the mistake, but later, they made sure to give me a hard time about it:

"You gonna join us for the whole number tonight, Kostroff?"

"Should we call a storm trooper rehearsal for ya'?"

"You have any other solos you want me to pick up?"

"Hey Kostroff, can you do my tap combination tonight? I wanna get a head start on my costume change."

Again, it's what we do.

Among the most famous mistakes in the folklore of *Les Misérables* is one that happened long before I joined the show. The villain of the piece, the intensely legalistic Inspector Javert, has infiltrated the rebel camp, claiming to be for their side. At this point in the show, he's just returned, he claims, from spying on the enemy. Following a tense, exciting, staccato musical introduction, he very rapidly gives his report. He sings:

"Listen, my friends. I have done as I said. I have been to their lines. I have counted each man. I will tell what I can."

Well, as the legend goes, one night, the actor playing Javert just went up* on all those words. And so, it came out something like this:

"Listen, my friends. I have been to their homes. I have watered their plants. I have fed all their cats. I have read all their mail . . ."

People who were there swear it's a true story.

Well, things happen. And God help you if you're onstage when a fellow performer loses it. It's hard not to laugh.

I still find it very strange that we could be so comfortable in front of an audience of thousands that we actually become distracted from the task at hand. But it happens. Sometimes, it's just another night at the office. And, as can happen at any job, our minds are occasionally on other things. Sometimes, we just plain space out.

When I was with *The Producers*, I'd find myself in the very same spot every night around 10:45 PM: high up on a stool behind my fake judge's bench, in the midst of the courtroom scene. It's rather a long scene, and I had only a few lines. Mostly, I sat there listening. I listened to Max plead his case, I listened to Leo plead Max's case, and then I listened while they both sang about it. Had you seen the show in month six or seven, you would have seen a judge who was deep in thought, seriously considering options. But if you could have listened in on my thoughts, you might have been surprised by what those options were:

"Let's see . . . I have a can of soup back at the hotel . . . that's not too bad. Or I could make a salad . . . What the hell: Taco Bell on

---

* *went up: "Going up" is theatre slang for forgetting your lines. If you're in rehearsal and an actor says, "Sorry. I'm up," it means he needs the stage manager to look up the line in the script and call it out. No such luck if you're in performance.*

the way home . . . Or maybe some of us will go out to eat . . . Nah, Taco Bell . . . Screw it . . ."

The night of the Tony Awards, *Les Misérables* was in . . . oh, who remembers what city? Fort Worth. That's it. Anyway. There was a *television set* tuned to the broadcast, at a very low volume–I swear to you–about *ten feet* from the down left entrance to the stage–*ten little feet* from all those singing Frenchmen. Whenever we weren't onstage, we were huddled around that set, straining to hear. Some members of the ensemble were even able to position themselves in such a way that they could see the TV screen *from* the stage. Can you imagine? Thousands in the audience, and they're sneaking peeks into the wings to see who won Best Use of Taffeta in a Musical.

Well, to be fair, the broadcast was particularly exciting this year because our own director, Jason Moore, was up for a Tony Award for his direction of the hit Broadway musical *Avenue Q.* Jason's a fantastic director, and we were all rooting for him to win. As the various results came in, we found ways to spread the news during the show. My trusty pad of paper once again came in handy as I distributed the latest results ("Best Book of a Musical–*Avenue Q*!! Up next: Best Leading Actress in a Play!") to my customers, who'd nod and smile and raise their glasses in tribute.

Sadly, Jason lost to another very talented director, Joe Mantello, who'd directed *Assassins.* The award was given out during a quiet scene at the barricade, in which our rebels are resting and regrouping for another day of battle. I saw one of these rebels ever so subtly cast his gaze into the wings. An offstage cast member shook his head with regret and then, with a psycho expression on his face, aimed an imaginary gun. Understanding this to be the sign for *Assassins,* the onstage rebel nodded sadly and began spreading the news.

Okay, so . . . now you know some of the secret goings-on of one particular Broadway tour. The sinful pleasures that happen in the dark. These are the things they don't teach you about in acting school. Then again, neither do they teach you how to sing while dragging a dead body, which two of us have to do nightly. I suppose that if there's any excuse, it's that when you do the same show night after night after night, you get a little numb. Maybe it's understandable that some of us, from time to time, might surrender to the silliness. Okay, some surrender nightly. Okay, fine, *some*—not I—aggressively look for opportunities to surrender. I guess messing around keeps them alert. Sometimes, the crew gets involved, the stage managers, even musicians. I suppose they're fighting the numbness as well.

But I think it should be noted that there's one group of people who are always excluded from the fun: the audience. The people *for whom we do the show*. The ones who paid the better part of a hundred bucks for each ticket, planned the evening, chose an outfit, hired a sitter, and came to the theatre to experience a wonderful evening of entertainment. In my heart of hearts, I really believe those people deserve better. So, while I myself have been guilty of breaking character and fooling around, I honestly don't approve of my own behavior on those occasions. It's like what St. Paul said about sin: "That which I hate, that do I do." After all, none of us got into theatre to *not* do the show. Surely, there's much deeper satisfaction and fulfillment and joy to be found in actually investing in the story than there is in making our cohorts laugh. And what's more, incidentally, it's our job the work we were hired to do.

I don't know what the proper balance is. No, that's a lie. Of course I do. We performers should always give the very best show we can, every show. At the very least, we should aspire to that. Personally, I'd like to demand more of myself, and adhere with firmer resolve to my own professional ethics, regardless of what's going on around me, or how late it is in the week.

The Brits have some great expressions for questionable onstage behavior. "Jiggery-pokery" is one of them. Literally, it means deceit, deception, slickness, and trickery. In theatre, it means mugging, hamming, and overacting. It has nothing whatsoever to do with this chapter. I mention it only because it's fun to say. Try it. I'll wait . . .

See? Jiggery-pokery, jiggery-pokery, jiggery-pokery. If you're not giggling yet, I don't know what to do with you. I give up.

But there is another British expression, one that means breaking character and laughing during a performance, and this is the more damning one. They call it "corpsing." It means that your character has died. Ceased to exist. By laughing onstage, you've destroyed the world in which he lives. You've killed him. As much as we may enjoy onstage antics, they really do dishonor our art. (Or "dishonour," as our friends across the pond would spell it.)

And yet . . . yes . . . there is still *another* side to this issue: Can the audience really tell?

There are those in my cast who would argue that it makes no difference whether or not we're in character, because the show works either way. And maybe they're right. There were many nights when, after putting in what I felt was a mediocre performance, I saw people weeping in the audience as they leapt to their feet. Grown men. Cynical, way-too-cool looking teens. Old women. Couples, holding each other. These people had been profoundly affected. And that's very humbling. Wait . . . I *think* that's why they were weeping. Shit. Maybe they just really hated my performance.

I once heard a wonderful story about Laurence Olivier, who is considered by many to be the greatest actor in recent memory. Sir Larry was doing a production of Shakespeare's *Titus Andronicus*. In a review of his opening night performance, a local critic raved about a particular moment in which Titus tenderly bids farewell to his own hand before chopping it off. Olivier, according to the report, made a meal out of that moment, caressing the hand, kissing it, burying his head in it, holding it, even turning away from view and whispering inaudibly to it, as if parting with a lover or a child. An amazing, riveting acting choice for him to have made. But as it turns out, it wasn't an acting choice at all . . .

Upon hearing of the review, Sir Olivier revealed the truth: The chopping-off-of-the-beloved-extremity effect was achieved with the help of some sort of mechanical apparatus attached to a fake hand. On opening night, this little contraption had gotten stuck somehow (in one version of the story, it was snagged on his costume) and Sir Larry was stalling for all he was worth while he tried to fix it unobtrusively. So, what looked like kissing was the poor genius trying to pull at the thing with his teeth, and the content of those inaudible whispers (and this is just my own conjecture) may have been something along the lines of, "Son of a bitch! What the hell's the matter with this cursed thing?" Or maybe even, "I could have gone into medicine or finance, but nooo. I had to be a fucking actor." Well, that's what *I'd* be muttering.

Meanwhile, the audience sat rapt, moved to silent tears by this stunningly theatrical moment.

I have no idea if the story is true, but I'd like to think it is.

The reality is that the emotional impact of theatre is sometimes achieved by accident, and often achieved by the viewer, who will probably never realize the extent to which he, using his imagination, subconsciously projects, interprets, enhances, and repairs our feeble attempts. Sometimes, good theatre happens in spite of us, the players, and regardless of our . . . "esprit de corpses."

Well, as you can see, I've had a lot of time on my hands here in Detroit to ponder these and other multisided questions. It makes for an interesting afternoon by the fire, safely tucked away in my great little hotel room, miles from the city, out on the road, somewhere in America, somewhere along my journey as a traveling theatrical.

Now, about those Chinese dumplings . . .

Kostroff

P.S. Jiggery-pokery! (Ah . . . it never gets old.)

20
IT'S DELOVELY, IT'S DELIGHTFUL, IT'S . . . DES MOINES?

January 9th, 2004

Hey there, my vicarious fellow travelers,

Have you ever seen those posters, "A New Yorker's View of the World"? They're these cartoony maps, drawn from a New York perspective, and they go something like this: the East River, then Lexington Avenue, Park Avenue, Fifth Avenue, Central Park, Columbus Avenue, Broadway, Riverside Drive, the Hudson River, New Jersey, the Midwest, Los Angeles, the Pacific Ocean, Asia, and finally, disappearing over the horizon, Europe.

And in some ways, that's really how we New Yorkers tend to see things. There's us, and then there are all those other little states and countries. I can't believe I'm going to say this, but New York is the Celine Dion of cities. We find ourselves completely fascinating. We love everything about ourselves, and assume that everyone else does too. After all, we're New York!

But being on the road, visiting all these places I'd never planned to visit, has really made it hard to sustain that view. Because I've discovered, to my complete shock—and you may want to sit down for this one—that many other U.S. cities actually have merit. Some of them even have—are you ready?—culture. Just between us, and please don't tell anyone that I told you this, there seem to be lots of smart, funny, hip, talented, interesting people who don't live in Manhattan. Weird, huh? Go figure. Well, anyway, all of this has really put a crimp in my New York snobbery, and I'm none too happy about it.

Des Moines, Iowa, I must reluctantly report, is a terrific town. It was rendered even more terrific by contrast with our last stop, Detroit. In fact, someone took to referring to Des Moines by the name "Not Detroit," as in, "Isn't it nice to be here in good old Not Detroit?"

It's cold, but we're used to that now. I bought myself a real, let's-get-down-to-business winter coat back at Filene's Basement in Boston for just eighty-five bucks: knee-length, down-filled, and made from the most synthetic materials available. It has an industrial-grade zipper, an enormous hood, and enough pulls and snaps to drive any gloved man insane. I honestly think someone could swing a lead pipe at me in that thing and I wouldn't feel it. Who knows? Maybe someone already did. I mean, we *were* in Detroit.

I hitched a ride here with Maria, one of the moms, and her son, Branden, who's in the show. (Branden spent the whole drive in the back of the minivan, watching DVDs and sleeping. Ah, to be nine again. What a life.) We drove straight through the night. I think it was around four in the morning when I happened to glance up at the on-board thermometer. It read . . . "3." That's right. Three little degrees. Just three. And the only thing separating us from the elements was this rolling metal box. As we pondered this, I thought about my friends back in LA, all happily snoring away in their nice warm beds as we barreled down that black highway in the dead of night in three-degree weather to get to our next tour stop. "Poor fools," I thought. "They don't know what they're missing."

About ten hours after leaving Detroit, we pulled up to the hotel in Des Moines, ready for hot showers and some real sleep. The hotel was every bit as nice as any at which we've stayed. Now, you've been traveling along with me, so by now you all know what's most important, and I can hear you asking: "Hey, Michael, does the bar serve food after the show?" Why, yes it does, thank you. They have a great late-night menu, served until midnight. *And* I was given a sprawling corner room where I could have easily given tennis lessons, *and* the theatre was just down the block. Since we're doing mostly one-weekers at this point, that kind of proximity has become especially valuable. For the most part, you really don't want to have to learn your way around.

Our audiences here have been warm and responsive and—here's the kicker—savvy. Des Moines gets all the Broadway tours, and they know what's good and what isn't. Yeah, that's right. They're theatre people. Deal with *that*, New York. Fortunately, *Les Mis* still plays beautifully wherever we go, and still has a powerful emotional effect, touching even the most sophisticated theatregoers. And even after all these months, I still can't believe I'm fortunate enough to be in the cast.

On opening night, we had an event in the lobby of the theatre! The choir from a local high school performed a medley of highlights from *Les Misérables*. Okay . . . truthfully? . . . I'm not sure how I feel about people hearing highlights from the show immediately before seeing it, especially because these rotten little bastards were brilliant, and there's just no call for that. I mean, why rub our noses in it, you know? Some of us sneaked into the lobby from backstage and hid around a corner to listen. Their diction alone put us to shame. And we had to *follow* these show-offs!

Later in the week, I was scheduled to speak at their school. They sang their *Les Misérables* medley again, just for me—a private concert! I was supposed to give them "pointers." I had nothin'. They were so terrific that I had to make things up. And yet they gawked at me in wide-eyed wonder, absorbing my every comment as if I were Itzhak Perlman showing them how to hold a violin.

As I've mentioned before in these reports, I really enjoy speaking to drama students and young aspiring actors. My hope is always that I can 1) dissuade some of them from pursuing this long shot of a profession, and

2) encourage those who truly have the calling, and can't be dissuaded. At the very least, I hope to give them all a more realistic picture of what an acting career is like. I often have to remind myself that some of these kids don't know how difficult it is to make a living in the arts. "Remember," I tell them, "you rarely hear about actors who aren't working. Mostly, you only hear about the very famous ones, and occasionally, about blue-collar actors like me. And I was only invited to speak here today because I'm currently employed. The reality is that *most* professional actors are *un*employed *most* of the time." A sobering thought, and a new one for many of them.

I love the questions they come up with:

"How much money do you make?" (The teachers are always more shocked than I am by that one.)

"What would you do if you were in a show and they made you dress like a girl?" (For some reason, this is the scenario that most terrifies junior high school boys. They're not sure what to say when I tell them that I've done it, and enjoyed it!)

"How do I get an agent?" (In *Des Moines*???)

"Can I get your autograph?" a sweet kid piped up.

"Of course! Come on up here."

As I signed his program from the show, he added, "You know. In case you ever make it." His teacher turned pale, but I wasn't insulted. He didn't mean anything by it.

I gave him a big smile. "Take a good look, my friend. This is it. *This* is making it. I'm employed! Very few actors become stars. I'm grateful just to earn a living."

Whenever and wherever I speak, I always include what I call my "commercial": a reminder about theatre etiquette—sadly, a dying art. I'm not sure how it happened, but in recent years, the tradition seems to be eroding. People arrive late, talk during the show, and sometimes worse. (Once, during *Les Mis*, a woman's cell phone rang right in the middle of the show's most tender moment, as Jean Valjean was writing out his last confession . . . AND SHE *ANSWERED* IT! Her shocked fellow patrons then overheard: "Hello? . . . At the show . . . Yeah, it's pretty good . . . lot of singing . . . What? . . . Well, he looks like he's about to die, so I should be home by around 11:30.")

So, I try to gently educate people whenever I can, not only about the rules, but also about the *reasons* behind them. I explain, for example, that talking while the houselights are down isn't only a non-negotiable no-no, it's *also* not the best way to enjoy a show. "It breaks the spell," I tell them. "Like if you were having a great dream, and someone shook you awake." I suggest that they get to the theatre long before show time and stay until the final curtain comes down, not only for the sake of etiquette, but also to get the fullest theatre-going experience—the most bang for their buck—all the way from exploring the lobby and reading the program to thanking the performers at the end of the play. Walking out during the curtain call, I explain, is like dining out and not leaving a tip for the waiter, and might make the performers feel that you didn't like the show. (I think people who aren't in theatre are often surprised to learn that we can see and hear them from the stage.)

Actually, I must say that I find theatre students to be among the *very best* theatregoers. They're involved, responsive, and into the experience. They dress up. They applaud generously. In fact, they're often among the diehards who linger till the end of the "Exit Music," when most of the audience has already left, to applaud for the orchestra. They set an excellent example for the grown-ups.

In spite of some of the serious content, my school visits tend to be casual, fun affairs. We chat about anything the kids can think of, and we always have a lot of laughs. Des Moines was no exception.

Speaking of the orchestra . . . If you've ever had any doubt that show people work hard, this item is for you: Larry Goldberg, our wonderful conductor, who has been suffering with a herniated disc in his neck, will be staying behind in Des Moines to have it treated as the show continues on with a temporary replacement. He herniated his disc . . . *conducting.* That's right. Most of us don't think of conducting as a physically taxing job, but it is. The repetition of those vigorous movements, with the arms held high enough for both musicians and actors to see, and the intense concentration of coordinating the entire pit with the entire stage, night after night, does not make one's neck, back, and shoulders happy. And *Les Misérables*, you'll recall, is all sung, top to bottom, all music all the time. So the one person who really doesn't get a break for three hours straight is the conductor. He can never put his arms down!

I say we make it an Olympic event. I'm sure it's a hell of a lot harder than some of those so-called sports, like badminton, or curling. Wouldn't that be hilarious . . . ?

> "*Blazenschmertz really needs to come through in these last few bars to make up for that botched sherzando section earlier in the piece, Dave.*"
>
> "*That's right, Jim. This is white-knuckle conducting if ever I've seen it. The Polish judge is particularly tough when it comes to cadenzas, but Blazenschmertz is showing no sign of strain as he rounds the bend into the coda.*"
>
> "*Well, he's been in training, and I think that shows.*"

Now *that's* a sport I'd watch.

Les Misérables isn't the only caravan in Des Moines this week. The Democratic presidential candidates are also here. We keep hoping to spot one, but it hasn't happened yet (though we did see a well-known newscaster at the bar). I suspect we keep very different hours. But it's wild to think that they're all *here*: Dean, Kerry, Edwards, Sharpton, all of them. And there's something so . . . I don't know . . . Fellini about the convergence of our two camps. Maybe it amuses me because of the sharp contrast: These guys are trying to become the friggin' president of the United States, you know? They're dealing with real, crucial, life-and-death, world-affecting issues. We're putting on funny clothes and singing. And yet, somehow, we all landed in Des Moines.

Lately, I've been hanging out with a great fellow cast member, Pierce Brandt. (He plays the frisky factory foreman who fires the fragile Fantine.)

Pierce is a very smart guy, and extremely gifted with language, which always skyrockets someone to the top of my list. We had lunch one day, then took a nice, chilly walk around town. As we crossed a bridge over a frozen river, something very natural and instinctive happened. We turned into little boys:

"Check it out!"

"Cool!"

"Hey! Let's climb down and *look* at it!"

"*Yeah*!!!"

We climbed down to the riverbank and studied the thin layer of ice. As is the male custom, we debated and exchanged theories on such matters as the thickness of the ice, the depth of the river, and how long it might take you to die if you were to fall in. And then we did what little boys do:

"Let's see if we can break it!"

"*Yeah*! I'll get a stick!"

"That stick's no good. *Here's* a good stick."

And that was our fun for the afternoon. Here we are, big successful grown-up working actors in a Broadway tour. But show us a frozen river, and we're kids again.

These one-weekers do tend to fly by. It feels like we just got here, and already it's nearly time to start packing . . . again. On Monday, we'll bus to Greenville, North Carolina, where, no doubt, there will be new stories to tell. Greenville, I hear, is a happening college town, with lots to see and do.

Still . . . I'm sure it's no Des Moines.

Stay in touch,
Kostroff

21
TALES OF THE HAUNTED SOUTH

January 26th, 2004

There are, among the traveling backstage crew of *Les Misérables*, men who have been on the road for years. Eight, twelve, fourteen years. These guys aren't flighty, sensitive actor types who deal in concepts and feelings. They're bikers. Drinkers. Guys with tattoos and long rock'n'roll hair. They smoke Marlboros, and they're not trying to quit. They have grown kids . . . somewhere. Sure, they're more intellectual and more sensitive than their carny roustabout predecessors, but still, these guys lift heavy things for a living, and often go days without sleep when the show moves to a new town. In fact, they're the ones who move it. They deal in solids and tangibles. And they've seen it all. For them, most of the theatres we visit are familiar territory, having played there before, and they know them inside and out.

So when Revo, the burly, grey-haired, Harley-driving tour veteran who operates the stage left half of the barricade, said to me:

"You know this theatre is haunted, right?"

I gave it special weight.

"Oh yeah. Guy died. During the renovation a few years back. Crew guy. Fell off the grid." He pointed to the slatted wooden floor way, way up above the stage, just below the ceiling. "Guy got impaled. Fell on the pin rail. There's still blood up there. He's around."

"Seriously? You believe in this stuff?"

"Well, I don't *not* believe in it. I've seen things."

Now, my attitude about ghosts is this: I don't believe in them, and I hope never to be proven wrong in that belief. I don't go looking for them, and I'd appreciate it if they'd stay away from me . . . if they exist . . . which I'm not saying they do.

But I do know that, according to experts on the subject, the presence of ghosts is often accompanied by mechanical failures and sudden drops in temperature. I also know that theatres are thought to be among the hauntedest places of all.

And so it was here in Greenville, North Carolina, at the Peace Center (which clearly wasn't named for the dearly departed crew member) that mechanical difficulties, both explainable and unexplainable, plagued the entire run, so much so that our stage manager, in his nightly written show report to the producers, included the comment: "Many of our company members have begun to believe the rumors that the theatre is haunted."

Now, our revolving turntable stage is *crucial* to the show. Everything–blocking, set changes, lighting–is designed around this particular device. All of the turntable's movements–its speed, number of revolutions, starting and ending points–are programmed into a computer, which is operated by Billy, our "automations" guy. Automations is a crew position which has become standard in today's highly motorized musicals. The automations person controls everything on the stage that moves automatically.

Well, on opening night in Greenville, the turntable went all screwy. Billy's computer lost its information, and stopped responding properly to commands. Onstage, we'd find ourselves moving when we shouldn't, or not moving when we should, or revolving right past where we were supposed to stop. Well, what the hell? We kept singing and made the most of it, while backstage, there was a mad scramble to troubleshoot the situation.

Finally, when a set piece failed to line up with its track, the stage manager had to make the difficult decision. He phoned the conductor in the pit and told him to stop playing. He announced over the backstage PA that we were holding. Meanwhile, Amanda, who plays Cosette, had been singing alone onstage. She heard the orchestra stop playing, and made a little curtsy, followed by her best attempt at a graceful exit. The curtain came down. Our ghost—if you believe in them, which I don't—had stopped the show.

"Ladies and gentlemen, we are experiencing technical difficulties. There will be a pause . . ."

Audiences love this stuff. Seriously. It's the story they can go home and tell their friends. Things like this make the evening even more of an event: "Well, we went to see *Las Miseryables*, and would you believe it, Madge? The turny thing got stuck right in the middle of the show and we had to wait while they fixed it! Isn't that exciting?!"

And to be honest, folks, people in a long-running theatre piece *also* love this stuff. It sure jazzes up the evening and breaks the monotony of what can become a fairly repetitive job. And so the news spread backstage like wildfire as half-dressed soldiers, whores, and magistrates watched suddenly busy crew members dash by: "We're going manual!"

Still relatively new in the show, and this being my first turntable breakdown, I had to ask: "What's 'going manual?' "

The turntable mechanism, I learned, has a backup. Billy sits at a button controlling the movements "manually" while the stage manager guides him via headset. (And you thought they had to get out onstage and push the darn thing, didn't you?) Every touch of the button moves the turntable forward. At certain points it has to be lined up precisely, which is tricky.

So after a brief, unplanned pause, we picked up where we'd left off, with Amanda bringing us right back into the story as if we'd never left it.

And for the rest of the show Billy had to sit, listening intently to the voice on his headset telling him, "a little more . . . a little more . . . stop!" as he deftly manipulated the green button on his console with a series of light taps. It was a long night for Billy. For those of us onstage, it was like sitting in two hours of rush-hour traffic: Go a few feet, stop, go another foot, stop, and try to avoid crashing into the guy in front of you.

We continued to have weird turntable malfunctions during the Greenville run. And as it turned out, that wasn't all . . .

There was a huge boom from backstage one night as a large, metal, garage-type door near the loading dock suddenly came crashing down, and spookily, none of those burly crew guys were able to get it open again. As chance would have it, the door landed on a crate, so they were still able to slip under it to get to where they needed to be.

Toward the end of another otherwise normal performance, as Jean Valjean was writing out his last confession before dying, his candle went out. There's no breeze in a theatre. Was someone reading over his shoulder?

Instead of the scrim that was supposed to come down from above the stage, a bridge, which wasn't supposed to appear until later, descended early during one show, nearly flattening our hero.

Another night, the sound engineer had *his* ghostly encounter as the effects for the big battle scene started going off in random order, forcing the onstage revolutionaries to improvise reactions to, among other things, an unexpected, and poorly timed, cannon blast. I don't think this dead guy likes musicals.

John, who operates the stage right half of the barricade, made an unexpected debut one night. He was engaged in his normal duty, moving a column onto the stage, when the column got stuck for a moment in the wings, delaying his entrance. By the time he got it on and locked it into place, the stage lights were up, and there was no way to exit without being seen, so he hid himself behind the column. What John had forgotten was that the entire stage was about to revolve. So, as Marius scrambled over the garden wall to be alone with Cosette, the couple, as well as the audience, discovered that they had company: a strange man in the garden, smack-dab in the midst of the lovers. He bowed curtly, and strode off.

The fact is, every department was affected by the ghost in one way or another, except for the wardrobe department, where everything was running smoothly. For some reason, they enjoyed an entirely haunt-free run. And then, on the very last day, during the load-out from the theatre, the wardrobe supervisor got hit in the head by a falling ladder. I guess the Greenville Ghost wasn't letting anyone leave without a reminder that he was there.

Our next stop was the very haunted Orpheum Theatre in Memphis, where paranormalists have identified no fewer than *eleven* different entities. The place was lousy with ghosts. But only one of them is so famous and widely acknowledged that she's featured in the official coffee-table book about the theatre:

Many years ago, a little girl named Mary was killed just outside the Orpheum. Mary loved the theatre. In fact, she was crossing the street on her way to a show when she was run down by a streetcar. They say she still attends every performance at the Orpheum, and that she always sits in one of the lower left box seats. If Mary doesn't like the show, she lets you know. Performers have reported looking up at that box during curtain call and seeing all the chairs facing away from the stage. That's Mary's equivalent of a bad review.

But what she *really* doesn't like is when a show uses those box seats to house speakers, equipment, or performers. This is what's not in the book. *The Lion King* had percussionists set up in that box, and they had the worst run of their whole tour. Our very own Revo was up there once, before he'd even heard the story, setting up equipment for another show. He says that in the center of the booth there was a circular area where the temperature was twenty degrees colder than anywhere else. He could step in and out of it and feel the difference.

And it was here at the Orpheum that, on the second night of the run, our turntable . . . well, this is how the stage manager put it . . . our turntable exploded. From what I hear, there were shooting sparks and loud pops and flaming wires involved. And the thing simply stopped working. In a case like this, there is no such thing as "going manual." The computer shuts down entirely, and the turntable is disabled.

"Ladies and gentlemen, we are experiencing technical difficulties. There will be a pause . . ."

Here we go again. This time, the audience was invited to take a break and stretch their legs. This was going to take a while. There is, I learned, a "Plan C": a backup turntable drive. But it takes a while to switch over. So, as the audience chattered in the lobby, enjoying what would now be the first of *two* intermissions that evening, wires were replaced and plugs were transferred. Ten or fifteen minutes later, after some test spins, we were up and running again. And, other than the show ending late, everything went fine for the rest of the evening.

We remained undisturbed after that. Maybe Mary decided she liked *Les Mis* after all. Even still, just between us, I will admit to you that I often glanced toward Mary's booth at curtain call to make sure the chairs were still facing the stage.

If ghosts exist, why do they like theatres so much? I posed this question to little Nadine, one of our young performers. She's nine, and when I asked her if she believed in ghosts, she got a big smile on her face and nodded emphatically. She liked the idea.

"So, here's my question: Do you think theatres are more haunted than other places?"

"Yes."

"And why do you think that is?"

"Well, maybe because a lot of theatres are old. So more things have happened there."

That made sense to me. And if I believed, which I'm not saying I do, I might also theorize that in a theatre, reality is shifty to begin with. What year is it? What's the season? Where are we in the universe? It all depends on the play. And maybe ghosts find, among the old props and costumes, reminders of the times in which they lived. Nadine thought that was a possibility too.

Another company member noted that theatre people, perhaps more than others, often suffer from unfulfilled dreams. Maybe they never got that great role, or the great love, or the great success for which they yearned. And so, they hang on, unable to rest, and mess with the rest of us. When I die, I wouldn't mind haunting a theatre or two. But I'm thinking my hang-out would be the chorus girls' dressing room. Hey, don't judge. To each ghost his own.

Every night, after the audience has shuffled out, and the actors have removed their make-up and changed back into their street clothes; after the ushers have picked up all the discarded programs, and the musicians have packed up their instruments, and the backstage computers have been shut down; when all the sounds of post-show chatter have drifted up the street and evaporated into the air, and everyone has gone home, a theatre falls into silence and darkness as it's locked up for the night. But before the last crew member exits, he places a single light on the stage—a bare bulb atop a metal stand. You've seen it in movies, whenever they have an onstage audition scene. That light is called a ghost light.

If it's true that theatres are more haunted than other places, maybe it's because here, spirits are honored. In fact, ghosts often appear onstage, as characters, portrayed by living representatives. Such plays as *Julius Caesar*, *Hamlet*, *Blithe Spirit*, *A Christmas Carol*, and notably, *Les Misérables*—to name only a few—all feature ghosts. (In the case of *Les Mis*, that's largely because almost everybody dies at some point, so it's either singing ghosts, or go home early and call it a night. There's even a version of the *Les Mis* tee shirt that reads, "It's not over till the dead lady sings.") Maybe ghosts haunt theatres because they feel welcome there.

Two quotes wrap up this report. One from Revo. He says:

"I never feel alone in a theatre. Not so much the new ones, but the old ones, definitely. Sometimes I'll know I'm the only living soul in the building, and yet I'll know for sure that I'm not alone."

And then there's this from Glenn in the prop department. He's one of the younger members of our crew, and a brilliant guy:

"You know, I believe in ghosts. But I also believe that when a turntable mechanism is fourteen years old, parts may need to be replaced."

I've encountered a number of mysteries in my time on the road. Like, why do hotels provide that little plastic bag to line the ice bucket? They don't line the water glasses, and you *drink* out of those. And why on earth do they always put the coffee maker in the *bathroom*? And whatever happened to that little sewing kit they used to give you? I liked those! Most of these mysteries will remain unsolved. But in the case of theatre ghosts, I think I'm perfectly happy not knowing.

Hope you're all in good spirits,
Kostroff

22

HOTEL/MOTEL/THEATRE/MALL

Unpack the luggage, la la la,
Pack up the luggage, la la la,
Unpack the luggage, la la la,
Hi-ho, the glamorous life!
—Stephen Sondheim, *A Little Night Music*

June 28th, 2004

Greetings from the road!

So many cities have flown by since the last time we all gathered here. And that's because as it is in life, so it is in touring: The longer you're around, the faster it all seems to go. And things are whipping by at such a rapid pace now, it looks like an old Keystone Kops movie.

There have been dozens of adventures since my last writing:

There was Memphis, where the famous Peabody Ducks live. Many years ago, a couple of drunken guests thought it might be funny to put live ducks in the fountain that dominates this grand old hotel's lobby. And they've been there ever since. The ducks. Not the drunks. They have their own room, in the penthouse, and every morning there's an official procession. A red carpet is rolled out, recorded music plays, and the Peabody Ducks emerge from the elevator to make their way to their daytime hang-out. They relax, splash around, and pose for photos until 5 PM, when there's another procession to return them to their lofty digs, where they retire for the evening. Okay. You doubt me? See for yourself: *www.peabodymemphis.com* (click "Vacation Guests," then "Duckling").

There was Columbia, South Carolina, where we once again crossed paths with the Democratic candidates for president. (Who's following whom, anyway?) One of the local dressers invited me to crash the debates with her, and though they were at—shudder—9:30 in the morning, I decided not to miss the once-in-a-lifetime chance to see the candidates live, and watch them interact with the locals. The dresser knew people at the theatre where the event was to take place, and they sneaked us in through the backstage entrance. Very educational experience. Another kind of theatre, you could say. This tough hometown audience wasn't lobbing any softballs, so the guys who fared well on TV didn't necessarily fare well here, and vice versa. Good old Al Sharpton, as always, came armed with a quiver of quips so incisive that you couldn't help but laugh. Here's my favorite: "Of *course* George Bush didn't feel he needed the U.N.'s permission to go to war! He didn't feel he needed the *U.S.'s* permission to become president!"

The last night of our run in Columbia also happened to be Super Bowl Sunday, and all through the show, the sports nuts in the cast, whenever they weren't onstage, had been running back to Inspector Javert's dressing room to watch the game on his portable TV. Scores had been whispered all night long during fast costume changes, and carried along the backstage hallways. The final update was actually delivered during the curtain call, as Javert himself came running out yelling, without moving his mouth, "Five seconds to go!!! Patriots kicking a field goal!!!" before taking his bow.

And there was Fort Worth, Texas, where we experienced the most outrageously dramatic, fantastic rain storm, which lasted for days, complete with glorious, heaven-shaking thunder and nearby bolts of sizzling lightning which, besides being a thrilling spectacle of nature's power, also became our second-rate hotel's catchall scapegoat for everything that went wrong. Me at the front desk:

"Hi. My key card doesn't seem to be working."

"Well, sir, it's the lightning. It erased all the computer codes."

"I see. Well, I also wanted to mention that both of the elevators are out."

"That's also because of the lightning."

"Really? And the lack of hot water?"

"Lightning."

"Cold food?"

"Definitely the lightning."

"Well, what about the ugly decor?"

"Again, the lightning. It hit the decorator in the brain and gave her real bad taste."

There was West Palm Beach, where we were close enough to my old *Producers* tour (they were in Ft. Lauderdale) that I was able to drive down in a rental car to see former cast mates on our night off. Lots of laughter and reminiscing all around. A group of us went to dinner, then crossed the street to the beach, where we shed our shoes and went for a nighttime wade in the ocean. The next day, Nancy and I lunched at a restaurant where tables and benches were mounted on big swinging platforms. You could eat and swing at the same time. And swing we did. This is the thing about touring. Would you ever even imagine such a place?

And then there was Tampa, where . . . well, perhaps a gentleman ought to leave Tampa out of it.

These places and these adventures, like slides in a slide show, like the landscape through the window of a moving train, blurring together in a cyclical pattern of repeating elements: hotel/motel/theatre/mall/airport/theatre/airport/stage/backstage/bus/hotel/stage/lobby/airport/lobby/backstage/onstage/airport/theatre/mall/theatre/hotel/airport/bus . . . and so on.

But now, we're preparing for the biggest adventure of all: the next chapter of our lives. At the end of our current engagement, in St. Paul, *Les Mis* goes on hiatus for the summer. And while some of us will return to the show in the fall, some of us will be moving on. Some have left this decision in the hands of fate—a.k.a. the show's producers. I've decided to call it a day, and return to the very different life of an LA TV actor. It's been . . . well, amazing, really. And I wouldn't want to take anything away from that statement by saying that I'm ready to be off the road. Both things are true.

And so we find ourselves in our final city as a cast. Our hotel is across the street from the water. On this tour, we've been lucky: We've often been by the water.

It's the home stretch. So people are breaking down a little. It's fine. We don't talk about it much. Par for the course.

In fact, some singers are extremely careful about discussing their vocal problems. Dancers, similarly, don't like to talk too much about injuries. And actors, as they get older, are reluctant to admit any difficulties they may have remembering lines. And there's a very good reason for these policies. A singer who can't sing, a dancer who can't dance, or an actor who can't remember his lines is useless. And news of any failings tends to circulate faster than bad jokes on the Internet. God bless showfolk. They do like to talk. So we protect ourselves by being somewhat secretive.

In 1992, for about two weeks while rehearsing a show, I had a mild, brief case of bursitis (a fancy name for a simple inflammation) in my knee. It passed, and everything was fine. *To this day*, people from that show will come up to me, with deeply concerned expressions that fail to hide their greedy lust for bad news, and ask, "How's the leg?"

"It's *fine*," I'll respond threateningly. "And it has been fine for over a decade. And if anyone asks, you may tell them there is *nothing* to worry about. Thank you for asking."

Why so defensive? Well, if word spreads about Michael and his non-existent "leg problem," then I might not be hired for my next job. So we're anxious to squelch rumors, and even facts, that suggest we're not at the top of our game.

I heard about a woman who received major critical acclaim for her brilliant portrayal of a wheelchair-bound character in a TV movie. After the show aired, she and her agent sat waiting for the offers to come in. They never came. Turned out that someone had started a rumor that she really was confined to a wheelchair, and everyone in Hollywood had believed it, and shied away from hiring her.

Animals in the wild will quickly abandon wounded members of the pack and leave them to die. Similarly, a cast will unconsciously isolate itself from a wounded performer. As if the injury were contagious.

Nevertheless, the truth is that from time to time, people in touring musicals do show the wear and tear of a constant schedule of beating ourselves up. It's a fact of life. We try to keep it a secret. We do our best to hide it. We do *not* baby ourselves. In fact, it's considered the height of weakness to miss performances because of some minor injury or vocal fatigue. Buck up. The show must go on. Theatre people really believe in that. It's part of the dancer's religion to simply pop a handful of Advil and get out there like everything's fine. When I tore my calf muscle in San Francisco, you can bet your ass I would have gone on, pain be damned, if I could have gotten my leg to move at all. We don't care about long-term damage. We don't care about pain. We only care about going on and doing the show.

Besides, there's always "Doctor Footlights." That's a performers' expression for the strange healing power of being onstage. Often, whatever is ailing us disappears long enough for us to do our jobs. Some say it's adrenaline, some say it's pure determination, and some say it's the sweating out of toxins under the hot lights. I prefer the mythology of "Doctor Footlights." I experienced it during a run of *Triumph of Love*, when I was so sick I could barely hold myself up (I'll spare you the details). I felt like death itself. But whenever I emerged onstage, I was singing and dancing and clowning for all I was worth. Then I'd exit, and collapse in a heap just barely out of sight of the audience. "How are you doing this?" asked a young performer in the cast.

"Doctor Footlights," I mumbled weakly, on the verge of passing out. It was as good an explanation as any.

Singers have a million tricks for singing over, around, through, or in spite of vocal challenges. And for most singers, it's always something: allergies, dryness, strain, acid reflux, something. And for these afflictions, we take . . . you name it: Claritin, Humibid, Zantac, Prevacid, Nexium, Advil (shrinks the vocal cords), Jolly Ranchers (they make you salivate), water by the gallon, Throat Coat tea—everyone has his favorite remedy. Some remedies are effective. Some provide only imaginary results, and sometimes that's enough.

As I said, this is usually handled in relative secret. But since it's just us, I'll confide this: On the final weekend before hiatus, some random and very stubborn gunk settled on my vocal cords, and none of my usual singer tricks were working. Unfortunately, I made the discovery during a performance—a singer's worst nightmare. Customers in the tavern scene looked at me as if to say, "What the hell is that coming out of your mouth?" It was funny, but frustrating. I just couldn't make the sounds, and it was getting worse. Back at the hotel, I tried steam, gargling with salt water, an expectorant, prayer, a decongestant, standing on my head (yes, really), you name it. No luck. I had to call out for the evening show.

I tried again to sing the next day. Nothing.

That evening was our final performance as a company. I waited until the last minute, hoping against hope that the frog would lift. Finally, it was 5 PM, and I had to make the decision. It just wasn't going to happen. My understudy, Chip, would close the run.

I could have gotten depressed about it, but what would have been the point? I simply couldn't do the show, and that was that. Determined to make the best of things, I decided that rather than sit in my hotel room and brood, I would head over to the theatre and watch the final performance from the wings, to feel that I was part of the event. I was going to make it a happy evening no matter what.

And then I had a small inspiration. One last bit of fun.

"Hi, Abra," I croaked, strolling into the company manager's office. "Do you have a copy of the instructions for filing for unemployment?"

"Sure. Here you go."

Using the copy machine, I reduced the one-page instruction sheet down and ran off a handful. I cut them to about four inches by six inches and wrote, "Happy Trails, from Kostroff" on the backs. Then, I attached them to the Thénardier pad, and positioned myself to watch what would have been my final tavern scene.

Chip, singing "Master of the House," began to distribute the bills. One by one, people turned them over, laughed, and raised their tankards in my direction. Some of them pretended to weep over the impending lack of work. Considering I couldn't be up there with them, it was a pretty good send-off.

"We have to stay in touch," Charlie said, hugging me after the show.

"That would be great," I said with a smile. I knew that wouldn't happen. It so rarely does. And I also knew that, at the moment, he meant that sentiment with all his heart. That's just the nature of this thing.

A few nights ago, I was at the theatre early, having felt a strong desire to spend a few moments alone on the stage to reflect before the show began. So I went out there, in my *Les Misérables* robe with my name on it, and just stood quietly, contemplating, as everything hummed around me. I listened to the warm murmur of the audience on the other side of the scrim, and the pre-show laughter of my show biz cohorts backstage. I looked at those beautiful scorched black cobblestones that make up the stage floor. Silently walked the circle of the turntable. Gazed up at the barricade. Touched the fake bricks. Looked up at the hidden lights that hung in the air overhead, past where the audience can see. The show looks so vast from out in the house. It's known as a "big" show. But to us, it's so little, this circle in a square where we go to work each night. It's lighting and smoke and, most of all, theatre magic that make it big.

"Well," I thought, "I did it. I got to the point in my life where I played Thénardier in *Les Misérables*. I managed to get cast in this wonderful show. That's something." And I felt soo, soo very lucky. "From here on," I thought, "everything is gravy."

And it is. I'll be returning to my great, funky little Hollywood apartment tomorrow, and to my own circle of friends, whom I've really missed, and to . . . the unknown, I guess, which is part of the actor's life. I've learned to embrace it, and even to be excited by it. Who knows what wonderful thing will happen next?

See a play, if you get a chance. See a good play. And when you do, know that we love putting it on for you. We live for it. So much so that we'll even do it sick or injured . . . if we can. It feeds us, electrifies us, makes us whole. Clap long and loud, and celebrate with us this ancient and still thrilling art.

By the way, before the rumors start, my voice will be back to normal in a few days, so back off!

Kostroff

EPILOGUE
(OR "THE CURTAIN CALLS")

December 11th, 2004

Lately, I've been missing the road.

It happens. This is how you know you have "the bug."

By the time *Les Misérables* closed for hiatus, I think most of us were truly burnt out. All those one-weekers. Tensions in the cast. Ailments. One too many French revolutions, and one too many choruses of "Do You Hear the People Sing?" The People were ready to go home.

When the cab dropped me off at my apartment in Hollywood, I felt like a soldier returning from the front lines of a war. Everything was exactly the same, except for the fact that everything was completely different. I wasn't the same man I was when I left. Life shapes you. Home at last. Thank God. Thank God. I was so relieved.

I sat, shell-shocked, staring, very, very still, very, very quiet, on my sofa. I felt like a drowning man who'd been washed ashore. I made no plans. At 8 PM every night, I looked at the clock. I played computer Scrabble. I channel-surfed. I did not sing. For the entire first week, I lived on whatever remained in the cupboard or freezer from before I'd left town. Canned soup. Crackers. Frozen pizza. After all that traveling, the journey to the kitchen and back to the living room was enough. The thought of venturing out to the grocery store made my brains hurt. I thought maybe I'd just never leave the house again.

By the second week, there was nothing left to eat, so I had no choice. I went out back and started my car. It coughed a bit before starting up.

It took me a while to come back to myself. But I was very happy to be done, for the moment, with road life. It was a win-win, really. I'd really loved being on the road, and really loved the two shows I did, and now, I really loved being home.

I had two offers to rejoin *The Producers*, and you can't imagine how tempting that was. I was so pleased to hear that they wanted me back. But I knew I needed a break. I knew that without question. I also knew I needed to re-cultivate the TV side of my career, or those casting folks would forget about me. It had already been two years.

It's now five months later, and I'm a very content fellow. Life *off* the road has been wonderful. I've been seeing friends, enjoying my apartment, wasting time, working on television again (miraculously, the casting people still remember me), and having a lot of success with some of my own projects. It's really good.

But I miss it. I miss the road. I knew I would.

Like so many things, road life looks much sexier with the blur of distance. I've forgotten the times I hated it. I've forgotten the loneliness, stupid fights with coworkers, the schlepping, the *Groundhog Day* factor. I only remember the fun. I only remember the outrageous joy of it. And all those thousands of people we entertained. And the camaraderie of showfolk. And the great, great honor and satisfaction of being an honest-to-God itinerant stage actor.

I'm working on learning vocal parts for an upcoming gig I have, singing backup. I grabbed an old cassette and taped my part so I could study it in the car. The other day I was driving somewhere, listening to the tape, practicing my harmonies. After the last song, the tape flipped automatically to the other side. And I heard myself, circa July 2002, in rehearsals for *The Producers*, working with the musical director on Max's big number, "Betrayed."

I let the tape play out as I reminisced.

In a few weeks, that same company of *The Producers*, my company, will be closing. It's not tragic. It's perfectly normal. But I decided, for nostalgia's sake, that I need to be there to see their last show. They'll be closing in Pittsburgh, which is where we opened. A perfect bookend. I want to be there.

There is no ending for this story. There can't be, really. Because theatre people—real theatre people—are insatiable. And I strongly suspect I'll be on the road again. "What's it like?" people frequently ask me. In these *Letters from Backstage*, I've tried to answer that question. It's like this: amazing, horrible, magical, thrilling, boring, tiring, energizing, satisfying, hilarious, sad, euphoric, lonely, fraternal, endlessly long, and far too brief, an adventure.

Really, there's just nothing like it.

Thanks for taking the journey with me.

Your traveling reporter,

Michael Kostroff

The Benedum Center. Closing day, January 30th, 2005.

ABOUT THE AUTHOR

ACTOR AND WRITER Michael Kostroff is a native New Yorker who now lives and works in Los Angeles. He was a member of the original cast of the first national tour of Mel Brooks' *The Producers*, understudying the lead role of Max Bialystock, and played Thénardier in the national tour of *Les Misérables*. Regionally, he's played Nathan Detroit in *Guys and Dolls*, Pseudolous in *A Funny Thing Happened on the Way to the Forum*, Milt in *Laughter on the 23rd Floor*, Herbie in *Gypsy*, and a host of other roles. He was nominated for an Ovation Award for his perform-

Photo: David LaPorte.

ance in *Immortality*, produced in Los Angeles by the Indecent Exposure theatre company.

Mr. Kostroff's numerous television appearances have included recurring roles and guest spots on such programs as *The West Wing, ER, The Geena Davis Show, King of Queens, Malcolm in the Middle*, and *The Steven Banks Show*, on which he played all of the supporting male roles. He's best known as the unscrupulous gang lawyer, Maurice Levy, on the HBO series, *The Wire*.

As a freelance writer, Mr. Kostroff has helped create live shows and special events for Disney, Buena Vista, Fox, and a wide variety of other clients. He's also written music, lyrics, stand-up comedy, cabaret material, and his own popular two-man show, *A Little Traveling Music.*

Letters from Backstage: The Adventures of a Touring Stage Actor is his first book.

Your comments and inquiries are welcome! Mr. Kostroff may be contacted directly via e-mail at BackstageLetters@aol.com, or by visiting the official Letters from Backstage *blog*: http://lettersfrombackstage.broadwayworld.com.

CREDITS

The Mary Tyler Moore sculpture is a TV Land Landmark, dedicated by the people of TV Land. Courtesy Greater Minneapolis Convention & Visitors Association.

"Goodbye"
Music and Lyrics by Mel Brooks
© Warner-Tamerlane Publishing Corp. All Rights Reserved. Used by Permission. Warner Bros. Publications U.S., Inc.

"Happy Trails"
Lyrics by Dale Evans Rogers
Used by Permission

"Kind of Woman"
Music and Lyrics by Stephen Schwartz
Used by Permission

"Prologue"
Music by Claude-Michel Schonberg
Lyrics by Alain Boublil & Herbert Kretzmer
© Alain Boublil Music Ltd. (ASCAP)
Used by Permission

"At the End of the Day"
Music by Claude-Michel Schonberg
Lyrics by Alain Boublil, Herbert Kretzmer, Jean-Marc Natel
© Alain Boublil Music Ltd. (ASCAP)
Used by Permission

"Master of the House"
Music by Claude-Michel Schonberg
Lyrics by Alain Boublil, Herbert Kretzmer, Jean-Marc Natel
© Alain Boublil Music Ltd. (ASCAP)
Used by Permission

"Javert's Arrival"
Music by Claude-Michel Schonberg
Lyrics by Alain Boublil, Herbert Kretzmer, Jean-Marc Natel
© Alain Boublil Music Ltd. (ASCAP)
Used by Permission

A Little Night Music
By: Stephen Sondheim
© 1973 (Renewed) Rilting Music, Inc. (ASCAP)
All Rights Administered by WB Music Corp.
All Rights Reserved. Used by Permission.
ALFRED PUBLISHING CO., INC., Miami, FL. 33014

INDEX

pseudonym

pseudonym

* *pseudonym*

Books from Allworth Press

Allworth Press is an imprint of Allworth Communications, Inc. Selected titles are listed below.

Making It on Broadway: Actors' Tales of Climbing to the Top
by David Wienir and Jodie Langel (paperback, 6 × 9, 288 pages, $19.95)

Acting–Advanced Techniques for the Actor, Director, and Teacher
by Terry Schreiber (paperback, 6 × 9, 256 pages, $19.95)

Improv for Actors
by Dan Diggles (paperback, 6 × 9, 246 pages, $19.95)

Movement for Actors
edited by Nicole Potter (paperback, 6 × 9, 288 pages, $19.95)

Acting for Film
by Cathy Haase (paperback, 6 × 9, 240 pages, $19.95)

Acting That Matters
by Barry Pineo (paperback, 5 1/2 × 8 1/2, 240 pages, $16.95)

Mastering Shakespeare: An Acting Class in Seven Scenes
by Scott Kaiser (paperback, 6 × 9, 256 pages, $19.95)

The Art of Auditioning
by Rob Decina (paperback, 6 × 9, 224 pages, $19.95)

An Actor's Guide–Making It in New York City
by Glenn Alterman (paperback, 6 × 9, 288 pages, $19.95)

Promoting Your Acting Career, Second Edition
by Glenn Alterman (paperback, 6 × 9, 256 pages, $19.95)

The Best Things Ever Said in the Dark:
The Wisest, Wittiest, Most Provocative Quotations from the Movies
by Bruce Adamson (7 1/2 × 7 1/2, 144 pages, $14.95)

Please write to request our free catalog. To order by credit card, call 1-800-491-2808 or send a check or money order to Allworth Press, 10 East 23rd Street, Suite 510, New York, NY 10010. Include $5 for shipping and handling for the first book ordered and $1 for each additional book. Ten dollars plus $1 for each additional book if ordering from Canada. New York State residents must add sales tax.

To see our complete catalog on the World Wide Web, or to order online, you can find us at
www.allworth.com.

CPSIA information can be obtained at www.ICGtesting.com
Printed in the USA
BVOW03s0212130813

328430BV00004B/8/P